Neighborhood Tales

Also by Norman Rosten

Poetry:

RETURN AGAIN, TRAVELER
THE FOURTH DECADE
THE BIG ROAD
SONGS FOR PATRICIA
THE PLANE AND THE SHADOW
THRIVE UPON THE ROCK
SELECTED POEMS

Fiction:

UNDER THE BOARDWALK
OVER AND OUT
LOVE IN ALL ITS DISGUISES

Plays:

MISTER JOHNSON
COME SLOWLY, EDEN

Nonfiction:

MARILYN: AN UNTOLD STORY

Neighborhood Tales

◆

by

Norman Rosten

George Braziller, Inc.
New York

Published in the United States in 1986
by George Braziller, Inc.

For information address the publisher:
George Braziller, Inc.
One Park Avenue
New York, New York 10016

Library of Congress Cataloging-in-Publication Data

Rosten, Norman
  Neighborhood tales.

  I. Title.
PS3535.0758N4   1986   823'.52   86–4189
ISBN 0–8076–1152–2

Printed in the United States
First printing, May 1986

Designed by Cynthia Hollandsworth

Contents

For Ann

Neighborhood Tales

◆

—being a compendium of happenings,
rumors, history, with real people and
events in the fictional pudding; an
entertainment born of a mythical place
anchored to the Brooklyn Bridge

The Poet Laureate

Early one morning I looked out of the window into my street. A clear cool spring morning. The sun already spreading its light over the rooftops, light leaping to catch trellis and facade of buildings, glinting upon cornices, and beyond my sight it touches the high stone towers of the nearby Brooklyn Bridge. I lean out, and to my left, a block away, the street shears off at the riveredge: across my vision hurries a harbor ferry. I see the city afloat on water, my daily glimpse of Venice. Brooklyn and Venice? An absurd connection. Yet beauty may strike anywhere on earth, then disappear with the blink of an eye. People meanwhile hurried toward the subway with the scrubbed look of early risers. Chatter of birds in the trees; the shouts of children echoed everywhere. A setting of idyllic calm.

Suddenly a voice could be heard above the hum of street activity, a resonant voice singing. A mechanical street sweeper came into view, driven by a young man who turned out to be the soloist. His head and upper torso leaned from the cab window as the vehicle swerved gaily around the corner, its two large rotary brushes whirling to attack the debris along the gutter. He was singing an Italian aria while he guided the sweeper against the curbside. (Where else such a moment but in Brooklyn?) A moment of the lyric beauty of man in harmony with Nature—except that his whirling brushes were whirling a foot or more above the ground. He had forgotten to lower them. He sang on, dreaming of his pension, as he accurately turned the corner, the street as dirty as before. No one cared, no one noticed, another day had begun.

An hour later the phone rang. A genial, carefree voice came in over the wire. "Good morning. Did I wake anyone? I'm only kidding. You writers stay up all night and never sleep. This is Howard Golden, and I hope this is Norman."

"Yes, and wide awake, Howard." The borough president and I were friends; we'd often meet dodging traffic, he hatless, I tieless, both breathless.

"Could I ask you to stop by this morning if not sooner?" he said with the air of a man guarding a secret.

"If you want the name of an agent—"

"No, I don't. I'm not ready for my memoirs. How about Borough Hall in say an hour? Some small matter. We can share a bagel."

"With coffee?"

"You got it."

(This is Brooklyn, where such things happen continually.)

Borough Hall, several blocks away, is a hometown touch of the classical, a landmark estranged from the standard architectural mix of the area. It adds nobility to an otherwise drab urban landscape, with the exception of the nearby federal post office building, a turn-of-the-century Romanesque favorite. As early as two years after this City Hall (as it was originally named) was built in 1849, a periodical commented disapprovingly of the "bricks and mortar, encroachments which are springing up on all sides, with magic rapidity."

Today, it remains a Greek Ionic structure throughout. The front portico is supported by six handsome Ionic columns with marble steps leading up from the street into the interior. A cupola, raised over the front center, is impressive, as is the whole, including the entire outer walls, formed of pure white marble. It may be Greek, but it has always seemed to me a mildly neglected Florentine palazzo. The regularity of the design (says my 1851 article) "is somewhat marred, we are constrained to say, by the windows of the upper floor being considerably less than those on the others."

I enter this historic building. Among its corridors and rooms, a century and a half of political hijinks took place, featuring wise men and clowns, honest men and thieves, scandal and serenity; at this time, one may see our leader Howard Golden, scooting about on serious business, with the bravura of an MC. Howard may come across as a football lineman, or

professor of paleontology, depending where you sit. He is a politician par
excellence, that is, he keeps getting reelected in a tough arena where
men are thrown to the lions daily. He is a handsome man (definite movie
possibilities), his charm runneth over; his one-liners spring from native
intelligence and good spirit; in short, a popular, pragmatic, jolly good
fellow, if his press releases are on the mark.

I pass an outside office of seekers: men, women, men with attaché cases,
men with beards and strange hats (Hasidim), men dressed well or in jeans,
women clutching notebooks or large manila envelopes—seekers of jobs,
favors, alleviation of pain, asking whatever minor gods can do to expedite
justice. But I do not wait. I am ushered into the spacious inner office
where Howard rises from his chair under the benign gaze of George
Washington, reaches over to shake my hand, and says, "I gave you one
spoon of sugar and some milk to kill the taste. Sit and try a bagel."

Seated across from his desk, I dip my bagel into the coffee cup with
precision. "How's the writing business?" he asks. "I hear the other
Norman"—he means Mailer, down the road apiece—"just got a million-
dollar contract."

"That was last week, Howie. It doesn't happen every week."

"I want to interest you in something much less. Very much less."

"I may as well finish the bagel."

"Enjoy. Meanwhile, a member of our staff thinks it might be a good
idea to appoint—hold on to your cup—a poet laureate for Brooklyn. I
don't know what that is exactly, but I like the sound of it. And you can
do it, he says. Murray Semach, he read your stuff and thinks you're great."

Once again, I hear the heavy knock of opportunity which can only
have unhappy results.

"There's no money in it, of course," he continues, "it's an honorary
thing, but we'll find something for you to do. Speaking for the borough,
I'd be honored if you'd accept. You've been a resident from way back,
written books and articles about the place, and Murray says you deserve
this dollar-a-year job."

"Can I think about it over a small nap?"

"Please." He smiled. "We'll have a regular induction ceremony before
the borough council and guests. We'll invite the press. A literary event.
Champagne, the works."

"Not even a part-time salary?"

"It would create problems, believe me."

"Would I have the use of an office, a secretary?"

"Maybe a work space, no secretary. It's a question of protocol."

"What about a parking space?"

"Absolutely not. I couldn't even get one for my daughter."

"I'll think about it."

"Personally, I'd be honored," he went on. "We need a little class in this administration. Murray says in England the poet laureate gets a case of port wine, plus some shillings for each year he serves. We'll certainly match that."

(This is Brooklyn, remember, where these things happen.)

"What are my duties without salary?"

"We're not sure. You can for example meet any VIPs who visit us. Or delegations. Foreign dignitaries. Attend official parties. You like girls, I hear. Also, you can write a poem for special occasions, like next year the Brooklyn Bridge centennial. Let me hear from you." He pushed back his chair. "Now I've got to face the mob in the next room waiting to lynch me."

I rose. "How can they lynch you? You're the sheriff."

"Except I lost my badge." Then, deadpan: "I want to thank you for coming and I hope it's been inspirational."

"The coffee was just right."

At the door, he said softly, "We've got a new receptionist. Give her a smile, she's homesick for the Bronx."

And so, for one dollar a year, plus the promise of a case of wine, I accepted the crown. (Actually, the ancient poet laureate was crowned with laurel leaves; if Murray knew about it, he never let on.)

The ceremony was impressive. In one of the large rotunda chambers of Borough Hall, several hundred people gathered, including politicos, assorted literati, local and out-of-town (Manhattan) reporters, and many of my own friends who perhaps saw me edging a toe into political waters. The place was noisy, flash cameras glinting; there was general good cheer. The day's business was coming to a close, and the laureate induction was about to move to center stage.

In the wings, wearing a new shirt and tie, I hear the chairman quiet the audience for my entrance. Lord knows what they expected. I was a writer in the community with a reputation and physical bearing continually confused with the other Norman, the one with money and wives. They wondered what's up. And I, waiting to go on, think, Is this where I am destined to be at this time of my life? Is this me singing an aria, my head in the clouds and the brushes spinning a foot above ground? Never mind why here or why Brooklyn, but why me? Seated next to me is Murray, the borough's unofficial historian and aide-de-camp, who cheers me on. "You deserve it, for one thing."

"It's a great idea, sure," I reply. "What a shame nobody thought of it earlier. This town had some important poets. Whitman, for example, what a laureate he'd make—"

"Yes, granted, but that's the nineteenth century."

"And you missed on Hart Crane, not to mention Marianne Moore."

"Is she alive?"

"She was fifteen years ago. Where were you?"

Murray shakes his head in dismay. "We're talking about today, not fifteen years ago, or five. You're a native, you're just down the block, you're a natural." He peers at me. "Are you backing out? What a hell of a time to back out!"

"Would I back out after I get into a clean shirt and tie, and get a haircut? I'm pleased to be the poet laureate, believe me, though the whole idea might be too rich for the masses."

Borough President Howard interrupts, leaning into the wings. "Let's go, fellas, while we got the crowd." With a grin, he says to me, "Don't get seasick. We just cleaned the place." I follow him back onto the stage where he's greeted with unruly but honest applause. As instructed, I sit on one of the dignitary chairs, alongside Murray and the county chairman of the Party. Howie is a great MC, born to the blarney, a politician in the best sense of that ill-famed word. He raises his hand for silence.

"I'm glad so many of you stayed for the high point of the day, the official welcome to the borough's first poet laureate. Some of you may say, who needs one? And I say, we do. Someone reminded me that Walt Whitman would have been a better choice. But we wanted a live poet, and Norman was available. And he's got the credentials. I don't know a sonnet from a haiku but I'm sure he does. He's promised as one of his first commissions to write a poem for the Bridge centennial. I think, in time, the people of Brooklyn will get used to the idea that a poet is watching them. So watch your step all of you out there. I'm proud to say that of the five, or is it six, boroughs of New York, we're the only one as of today with a real poet laureate, even though it took us a long time to get around to it." Then, he turns to me. "Welcome. Whatever you do, and we'll try to find work for you here, may you be successful. The only thing I ask is that you don't one day run against me for office. Who knows, maybe a poet would make this city work. And now, so you won't go away empty, or enriched either, here, in advance, your yearly honorarium, one dollar." He holds up the bill. The audience applauds. "Next year we might raise it to two, if the budget allows. The point is, my friends, money is not the point. The poet does things for beauty, though I'm sure he can pick a winning horse if necessary to pay the rent. I also give him, along with the symbolic dollar a bottle of sherry, in the English tradition." He hands me the bottle, wrapped in silver foil. Cheers rising out front. "Maybe next year we'll make it a case. And now, I hope the writer can give us a few of his words."

I step forward, holding the bottle and the dollar. "Every true writer knows that man does not live by beauty alone, so I welcome money and drink in moderation. That said, I accept this honorary post, whatever my duties turn out to be. May they be small ones. And within reason. I ask Howard not to wake me in the middle of the night saying he needs a poem by morning for his daughter's graduation. I won't do that, Howard! But if an Arabian or any other beautiful princess is passing through on the way to an official visit to Manhattan, and we need a passing sonnet for the occasion, you can wake me for that. I insist you do. I can, if requested, open a meeting of your Board of Estimate with the reading of a poem. I won't do any of this often, so relax. May I leave you with a thought by a man whose name we mentioned here earlier. His is the most honored name from our borough, Walt Whitman, truly the first poet laureate of our country. He said in an essay about America a century ago, this man who lived and worked just a few blocks from here, 'For so long as the spirit is not changed, any change of appearance is of no avail.' He was telling us to look inward, and forget about a new shirt and tie. Thank you."

There was silence, unexpected and ghostly, in that large hall. What had I said? Had I touched something too serious for the occasion? Then the applause rose up, and the ceremony was over.

Howard shook my hand until I winced. "You were great, kid. Everything you said."

I had the dollar folded in my hand. "How about autographing the famous dollar, Howie?" With a borrowed pen, he leaned on the podium and scrawled upon the bill, *Hail the poet laur* . . . "How do you spell that word?" He winked and finished signing. A small rush of friends and well-wishers swelled up around us. The party spilled into an adjoining room where tables were set up with dozens of glasses sparkling and ready for use.

"Can I kiss the poet laureate?" a woman standing nearby asked Howard.

"Of course," he replied. "But only if you live in Brooklyn."

Lady Anonymous kissed me and moved on to the drinks.

"Follow me," Howard commanded. "I understand you're a chocolate freak." In the far corner of the room, sat an enormous chocolate cake, easily three feet square, emblazoned with pink and green lettering: *Brooklyn Welcomes You.* Poetry and chocolate merged into symbolic unity.

"Cut yourself a slice," said Howie.

"After you, ole Prez," I said.

"Let me, let me," called out the woman who kissed the laureate. She picked up the knife and cut the first three slices, one for me, one for the borough president, the last for herself. The knife was then passed around, and more slices were cut in earnest, with barely a dent in the three-by-three foot cake, or was it four-by-four?

There were several impromptu toasts in my behalf; I may have offered one myself under the influence of chocolate. Within an hour, most of the crowd had gone. The caterers had started to clean up. Howard and others of the official party prepared to leave while I stuffed myself in a manner unbecoming a man with new responsibilities.

Howard came over and again shook my hand. "I was proud of you up there. We're glad to have you on the team."

15

"Thanks, Howie. I liked your speech too."

"I'm going to brush up on this guy Whitman."

"Did you know he was an editor on the old *Brooklyn Eagle* for a while, the old beard himself, imagine?"

"Anybody who did any good once lived here, it's a fact," Howard said. And he meant it.

I washed down some cake with champagne. "By the way, what happens to this cake, what's left of it, when we leave?"

"What do you mean, what happens?"

"It can't all be eaten."

"They walk off with it, whoever, we don't keep track." He leaned closer. "Go ahead, you want it? I'll turn my back. Better still, I'll wrap it for you, how about it?" He found several plastic bags and carefully fitted the slabs of cake into them. "Better the laureate steals than the cleanup crew. Go, live it up, and think of your first official poem!" We embraced like two generals in an old Russian movie.

Out in the street, armed with a title of no practical value, and carrying ten—twenty?—pounds of chocolate cake, I wondered if my darling fates had meant this day as a warning. If asleep, must I wake? If awake, must I know where I'm going?

I wait for the light to change. An image leaps to mind of a driver rounding the corner in his street sweeper, a song at his lips, joy in his heart . . . with the rotary brushes off the ground and useless. I lean against the light post and hear someone laughing. It must be me.

Brooklyn and
Whitman's Ghost

Spending half one's lifetime in a neighborhood that echoes the Whitman legend is not a bad fate for a poet. For some thirty-five years I have roamed the streets of Brooklyn Heights, those same streets he once roamed. I would see his image in any bearded burly sunburnt passerby along the old trolley tracks (long since gone) of Adams Street, a stone's throw from the once-standing offices of the *Brooklyn Eagle*, which Walt Whitman edited back in 1846. For decades, I couldn't pass that area without a tremor of mystic connection. He wrote: "Arouse! for you must justify me." How I yearned to! He wrote: "If you want me again look for me under your bootsoles." Being young, I looked, and pondered, and loved the man.

I would often pass a low-structured two-story red brick house on the corner of Fulton and Cranberry where, in 1855, in the offices of Rome Brothers Printing Shop, the poet hand-set much of the type and printed at his own expense the first copies of *Leaves of Grass*.

A century later, the real estate developers bought up the small homes and shops that lined Fulton Street from Montague to the foot of the Brooklyn Bridge. The song of the bulldozer was heard upon the land. Urban Renewal, a new media word, later to become known as gentrification, decimated the area. Left standing for a tantalizing period was the little Whitman house, the lower floor a rather seedy luncheonette, which remained the last barrier in the path of the Cadman Plaza Title I project. A group of local citizens who knew that Whitman was more than a brand name for chocolates decided to put up a fight to save that building, led by myself and the Rev. William Glenesk of the Spenser Memorial Church. The Historical Preservation movement had not yet arrived and the battle was a losing one. I was a step ahead of the bulldozers and managed to save some of the original bricks. Today, we have a high-rise complex with the fashionable address of Whitman Close. People love it.

Even as Whitman surmounted cynicism, so must his admirers and followers. I am his follower. Growing up in the Thirties, with its own Horsemen of the Apocalypse—Depression, Hitler, and War—many a young poet, including myself, was drawn to our contemporary Carl Sandburg and granddaddy Whitman. These were the bedrock poets of cities, the movement of peoples, political hopes and elegies. No metaphysical entanglements of Wallace Stevens or e.e. cummings in the decade of hard times. (We would correct that prejudice later on.) The key words then were "social consciousness," meaning an all-embracing sense of society. Whitman had this consciousness. He wrote about America as no one had before. As a poet of a developing democratic society, he appealed to our own idealism of a better world to come. His naiveté is matched by ours, but his vision is beyond ours.

Though Whitman understood the corruption inherent in democracy, his work retains that power of optimism rooted in the endurance of the American idea. He spoke of America as "Daughter of a physical revolution—mother of true revolutions, which are of the interior life, and of the arts." He reminds us of what we must yet become.

On bad days he is my rock. I see him in our Elysian fields (just off the Brooklyn-Queens Expressway, Canarsie exit) enjoying the weather, inviting his soul, chatting with new arrivals, rebuking local poet Hart Crane for excessive rhetoric and Marianne Moore for too much fancy skiprope, reminding them that poetry can be both simple and ecstatic. "I stand in my place with my own day here," his voice booms out, "underfoot the divine soil, overhead the sun."

Or if I want a more tangible contact, I stop by the Historical Society on Pierrepont Street and read from his two letters in the manuscript collection. One, dated Brooklyn, January 15, 1849, is a brief plea to a client regarding an overdue bill "so that I could get my pay as quickly as possible—For like most printers, I am horribly in need of cash."

Just to let you know, Walt, things haven't changed much for poets. But we have your presence, your shadow touches us still.

Landmarks from the Window

A tree growing in Brooklyn is somehow more appealing than a tree anywhere else, as novelist Betty Smith once discovered. Of course, the idea of a tree in any densely urban area is awe-inspiring: the courage, the daring, blindly asserting itself into poisoned air, attacked by dirt, dogs, mischievous children, careening motorists, lovers with pen knives.

A solitary tree on a city street has a greater impact than a forest. The tree, multiplied, becomes a forest, while a diminished forest can never become a tree. The single tree, even one on each block, would be a treasure. We treasure what we have least of, be it time or greenery. How poignant to see a young sapling wired into ground supports, braving the wind: I never pass one without whispering "good luck."

With leaves trailing earthward, those bare trees prepare for winter with all of nature's bravado. Surely part of our human optimism arises from our knowledge that spring is ahead, and with it the return of that green branch of life.

My own life has had its share of tree drama. Recently, a lowly ailanthus (the original tree which grew in B), having greeted me at my second-story window every morning for years, chose one morning not to appear. One evening, it was there; next morning, gone. To further the mystery, its roots were in the adjoining yard, while the leafy crown arched over a high fence to reach my window. It had been cut down. How? By whom? Was it an act of vandalism or theft? Who would want to steal a tree? I cursed the world, and went into mourning.

However, there was another tree in my life at that same time, a backup tree, a young willow in the other adjoining yard. Year after year its leaves flourished and faded, to cling tenaciously into cooler autumn weather and fall only with the frost. I would study that tree with the seasons, and the days, in light and shade, as obsessively as Monet his water lilies. Willow and ailanthus were my landmarks from the window.

With the ailanthus gone, I had the comfort of the willow. I soon forgot the loss of one for the radiance of the other. Until one day I awoke from an afternoon nap to the rasp of a power-saw outside. A repair crew, I thought, engaged upon good civic work. Later, glancing out the window, I could hardly believe it—the willow was gone! My solace, my beauty, my tree, vanished.

I brooded over the inhumanity of man, more specifically, my new neighbor. The idea of a city dweller cutting down a tree (in broad daylight, without shame!) was almost too much to bear. Each morning of the week that followed I looked to the garden where my willow once lived. Yes, *my willow*, for is not possession in the eye of the the beholder? A museum may own a work of art, but I "own" it when standing before the canvas; its inherent beauty is given to me at that moment. So it was with my willow.

My misanthropic juices flowed. I was ready to leave the city forever. Soon after I met my next-door neighbor on the street. I greeted her with a blunt: "What happened? Why did you cut it down? I'm not exactly a stranger to the tree. I live next door."

"You're the writer, aren't you?"

"Yes." (A reader: was it possible for her to love a book and hate a tree?) Though warmed by her recognition, I did not smile.

"I know how you must feel," she continued. "Would you believe it, I've received a dozen calls from people whose windows look out over my garden. They've all made inquiries about that tree." She went on to say she had been accused of negligence; others offered condolences; all were unhappy and even angry that it was gone. "I'm sorry it had to be done. I had no idea it was so popular. I'm still amazed that it touched so many people."

She then explained that the willow had been struck by a disease, and was removed because of the insects that swarmed over it. Would I be pleased to know that another tree was soon to replace the missing one? I would.

I said that I appreciated her generosity and concern. Would she accept a book as a token of this appreciation? She would.

Today, I look out at my landscape. It's there, not a willow, nor an ailanthus, but something resembling a dark-leaved maple. I'm at peace again. One tree, one backyard, one city.

The Lunch Club

The other Norman and the singular David (Levine) and I liken ourselves to a raggy sort of Three Musketeers, good companions of the neighborhood and possibly happy souls when the weather's right. We sometimes lunch at the Greek place on the corner when our cycles of work and sloth can be juggled.

Norman, the Other, needs no introduction, which means, aside from his bulk, he would be difficult to describe. His movements seem to emerge from certain psychic impulses. If he walks with a springy step, he may be dodging an ominous thought; a slouch may indicate oncoming paranoia. Time has slackened him a bit. L'enfant terrible is showing signs of le tigre doux. But let no man misjudge his present quietude: this volcano has some jolts left for the surrounding countryside. His scars are honorable and well earned.

David, the One, less volatile and weighty than N, gives off an easy, non-violent glow, yet could be plotting grave crimes. He appears lazy; not so, he may be simply a man of appearances. An artist who does as much cross-hatching as D is definitely a chameleon, which means he is subject to multiple interpretations. Lunching with these two gentlemen is therefore fraught with unpredictable possibilities. While we come together in peace, we often leave in confusion.

At times, our lunch a trois becomes a deux, as either the other N or the original D drops out at the last moment. I never drop out. My life style, casual and non-competitive, is rarely interrupted. If N drops out, D and I talk with some passion about the corruption of writing, art, and mankind in general; when D is missing, the other N and I put our intense heads together and come up with lots of halfass dialogue probably worth a fortune. When all three show up, wisdom crackles above our booth like lightning.

David will say, "Critics talk about my political cartoons because they don't know how to talk about my paintings. When pressed, they point to my watercolors but don't see my paintings. Why? I never went through the abstract salami machine and they won't forgive that. I stayed with figures, human faces."

I will say, "I received an incredible royalty check in the mail yesterday. Shook me to my handball shoes. Check for $7.90. How, you may wonder? It seems that ten years ago a German composer translated and set to music a short lyric of mine. It finally got on a record with twenty other snippets by others. Voilà: $7.90. It adds up, friends."

The other Norman will say, "It's tough on good writers who'll never find their reading public. They're doomed not to get picked up by the big PR floodlights. I feel bad about that. I know some of those guys. Because a few like myself draw off the big advances, and get the hype and headlines, the others get shut out. And they're talented as hell. The publishers don't give a damn. Maybe none of us do. Pass the mustard."

Our long friendship may be sustained by each of us feeling he is not threatened by the others. David and I give the other Norman, king novelist of the hill and terror of the streets, his reign; we do not poach on his territory, we're too smart. David, being one of the best caricaturists in America, and an excellent painter, is no threat to us Normans. While the other Norman has done some wild impromptu pen drawings (one a self-portrait drawn in my presence, entitled "Norman Mailer getting a brain wave while listening to Norman Rosten," I shall one day put up for auction with a floor of $250,000—you can't sell two Normans for less), he is hardly a threat to David's hegemony. David, however, is full of ingenious literary ideas and has more than once enticed me into developing them, but I see no threat there except old-fashioned enterprise. And the other N has even praised me on occasion; he wrote a jacket blurb for my second novel that I to this day consider the high point of the book. I tell people to read his blurb and feel free to stop there.

I believe we have respect for one another, and a silent praise. We meet, slide heavily into the Greek booth, consult the menu and take our chances. We exchange information and gossip but probably save the best stuff for ourselves. David may talk of a recent visit to Coney Island, its people already immortalized in his watercolors. David has been a Coney voyeur all of his life; he is the Daumier of beach people. He may also suggest a good story idea for me to develop; of late I pretend to be studying the menu and give him a *nolo contendere*. When pressed, he will speak of painting, or a European exhibit, or the possible origin of Mona Lisa's smile: is she going to her psychiatrist, a rendezvous with a lover, or is it a digestive rumble?

On the subject of women, the other Norman is very low-key. And why not, I think, when he has his high-key lady Norris at home? What might surprise the eavesdropper is that what we want, two hungry writers and a painter, is food; talk of sex would be a distraction. Whatever such talk there is would hardly interest the reader, such heady stuff as whether there is good or bad nudity and did anybody care so long as it was cheap and available—strictly sexist stuff to ease our morning chores and take our minds off money. Money is the eternal thorn. Living a notch or two above the poverty level (I won't go into the advantages; nobody would believe me), I'm both fascinated and bored as the other two kick the subject around. David is screwed somewhere on his subsidiary rights, or calendar rights, losing X number of bucks, while the other Norman is always caught in the snares of a complicated contract, with subsequent losses, etc.

I say, "All you guys do when we meet is talk about money."

The other N replies, "It could mean we don't want to talk about writing or women."

"Why don't we?" I insist.

"Because," says the master, "they're not good campfire subjects, and they don't go together. And either alone is too big to wrestle with at lunch. To get mauled you have to go into the lion's den, which covers both writing and women. As a metaphor." Or words to that effect.

"Did you gentlemen hear about my new theory predicting Russian changes in leadership?" asks David. "I call it the hirsute plan. Hair, comrades. Start with Lenin, the first leader. Bald. Impassioned but definitely bald. After him came, you guessed it, Stalin. Hair, lots of hair. Exit Stalin, enter Kruschev. Bald again. Followed by hair. Next is bald.

I could make a fortune if I knew how to market it. Dialectical materialism is based . . . on hair!"

The waitress brings the food, leaning over the table in a manner that prompts more sexist talk. It bores the lady; we don't look like good tippers anyway. The other N is the only really recognizable celebrity here, and the financial word on him is negative; even the waitress knows about his wives and his alimony. Everyone knows he's a hard worker and contract-poor. So the meeting turns out to be about food, money, and sex, in that order of importance. Literature and art are mentioned in passing. This is not quite the stardust stuff of *People* magazine. The other Norman is a cantankerous fellow, lately a devoted family man with an understanding wife; David is a mellow neighborhood wit, absolved of scandal; I am the poet in an ancient apartment coveted by the landlord. What else is there to say for the multitude? David suggests a possible change of venue for the next lunch club session. He mentions Burger King.

"Burger King!" Both Normans are alarmed.

David is calm (he always appears calm, by the way). He says, "Gentlemen, ask yourselves: why do you feel at ease in this Greek dive or a Chinese joint or Hungarian fast food, and cringe at the mention of Burger King? It's snobbery. Elitism. You want to avoid the poor. Could it be a pinch of racism, ha ha? Very possibly. But you're missing the point. Burger King is a throwback to a great American institution: the Cafeteria. Remember Stewart's or Horn and Hardart and so many other wonderful places before this town was gentrified out of existence, where you could sit at a table with a cup of coffee and a friend or two and talk? Stay for an hour, an afternoon, a day if you liked. Women brought their kids, who ran around wildly. There was the sight and smell of humanity. There's a little of that spirit left at Burger King. Elsewhere, what have we got? Eat and run, or eat and be gently reminded to run. By the way, no waiters, no tips, and a great salad bar. Do I hear a unanimous aye?"

With a roguish smile, the other Norman says, "It sounds like an existential experience, a proletarian throwback, or both."

I say, "How about a test run, myself and a friend, or a wife, or both. I'll report and then we can vote."

"Tabled until the next meeting," intones David.

"Are we going to take up the matter of opening the club to women?" I ask.

A silence. "Toil and trouble," mumbles the other Norman.

"Tabled until the next meeting," says the wise David.

"You're cowards," I say.

On several occasions, when D didn't show up and the place was crowded, the other N and I walked from the Greek's to a nearby Chinese restaurant. He liked the window view, one flight up. From there, we both looked down upon the busy small-town street (Montague). We ordered one of the specials, soup included. Next we surveyed the scene below, with nostalgic comments on the women who passed, the emphasis more on beauty and grace than carnality. After his six wives and my one, we still had an eye for the women, which we compared to a cosmic imperative. He marveled at his numerous marriages compared to my single and long-term love. We weren't sure what that meant precisely, except he surmised I knew something he didn't, or that my wife was the one who knew it. Whatever it was, he thought I was lucky. We read our fortune-cookie messages; he wondered if Wittgenstein might have written some of them while I suggested a defrocked Haiku master or Dr. Joyce Brothers. We exchanged our messages and they seemed to work as well with their new recipients. On such days, he was engaging and relaxed, good company for lunches or literature.

In this instance, he suggested dinner one day soon at his place, with Norris cooking, and the other poet, son John Buffalo, age six, exhibiting his new poem entitled "Money."

"The kid's got the right instinct," he said with a grin. "But I don't see him as a competitor, you've got nothing to worry about. He'd get a kick out of reading it to you."

"All right. Set the date."

We split the check, as befits any two Normans.

What's So Funny About Brooklyn?

What have Woody Allen and Barbra Streisand in common? Or Jackie Gleason and Harry Golden? Elliott Gould and Neil Diamond? Danny Kaye and David Levine? Norman Mailer and Susan Hayward? Rickles and Cosell? Buddy Rich and Vic Damone and Lena Horne and Arthur Miller? As well as Buddy Hackett, Mickey Rooney and Phil Silvers and Abe Burrows and Anita Loos, Lillian Hellman, Ira Wallach, Henry Miller, Irwin Shaw, may as well mention Norman Rosten....

I could go on, but you deserve an answer. Those above-mentioned, and dozens of other celebrities, thinkers, entertainers, were either born or spent their formative years in Brooklyn.

Brooklyn. Over the Bridge. The Badlands. Bedlam in Bed-Stuy. Coney Island. The original home of Nathan's Famous Frankfurters. Where once the Brooklyn Dodgers smote the enemy at the Field of Ebbets (long since fled to Los Angeles and eternal shame), and where Jackie Robinson broke the Big League color barrier at second base. Where The Tree That Grew was planted. Where the first taxi driver is supposed to have come from, brandishing his Good Elocution Certificate.

Brooklyn is a place people fight to get out of and, once out and having tasted the rest of the city (or world), fight to get back into. By that time, someone may have stolen his or her car or parking space. I know of writers who went to pieces when they left the holy sod.

Brooklyn (let me go on) is a name that brings the most amazing variety of emotions to the surface. At its mere mention, I have seen people smile, groan, look suspicious, back away a step, embrace me, threaten me, pass a hand unsteadily across their faces, weep, stutter, or fall into a trance.

I met a man in a Nome, Alaska, bar who bought me a drink because I was from Brooklyn. No other reason.

I met a woman who suggested a liaison because I was from Brooklyn. No other reason.

Another woman confided to me that her daughter was about to marry a native Brooklynite who, she hoped, would be kind to her. No other reason why he should be or shouldn't.

A pedestrian shouted at me from a street in New Jersey as I made a sharp turn: "Where'd you learn how to drive—in Brooklyn?" (How did he know?)

A sentence scrawled on a Manhattan subway poster: "Brooklyn is under water."

A friendly poet from San Francisco writes: "I have just written a Brooklyn poem," and sends it along, to wit, or half-wit:

> In de spring the poet sings,
> He says de boid is on de wing.
> Upon my woid that is absoid
> Because de wing is on de boid.

Brooklyn, what sins have been committed in thy name! Funny stories, idiot jokes, a leer, a smirk at the mention of your holy syllables! Yet you are as innocent as the falling snow. Well, at least as innocent as the Bronx, or Queens, about which people say nothing, good or bad. Why do people pick on my hometown? Jealousy? Hatred? Greed? Because we have hills? (Yes, we do.)

I blame most of this bad folklore upon the old World War II movies. For some reason (do we need a reason?) Hollywood needed a buffoon image, a pratfall guy, and some genius writer or producer invented a Brooklyn taxi driver who was drafted into the Army. Naturally, he could drive a tank blindfolded. Naturally, he was the dumb guy whom everybody joked about, but who always did something heroic by accident, maybe even died. The Brooklyn boy became the village idiot of show biz. All over the world, wherever our cinema culture surfaced, gullible foreigners learned to laugh at the slob from Brooklyn. This mass delusion is waning only because other mass delusions are more promising.

Actually, Brooklyn has always attracted good, decent, curious, intelligent people. You didn't have to be born here to be lured over. Heywood Broun, George Gershwin, Theodore Dreiser, Norma Talmadge walked or sat here. Mae West, Houdini, Betty Smith, Thomas Wolfe, S. J. Perelman also slept here for some part of their lives. Marilyn Monroe slept here—in fact she slept in my house.

To get back a bit. George Washington visited, but didn't stay long, retreating not by choice but military necessity. Henry Ward Beecher preached his anti-slavery sermons here. During the mid nineteenth century, Brooklyn's showplace was Coney Island, and into the borough on a Sunday several hundred carriages could be seen driving southward over grassy meadows (the Brooklyn–Queens Expressway wasn't invented yet) where, at the fashionable Coney Island House, for example, the registered guests included such luminaries as Herman Melville, Edgar Allan Poe, Jenny Lind, P. T. Barnum, Daniel Webster, Henry Clay, and Washington Irving. Another hotel, called the Ocean Pavilion, could entertain 20,000 guests and bragged of a ballroom where 3,000 dancers could glide beneath 400 gas jets. Brooklyn, a century ago, seemed pretty lively, causing a visiting Cuban patriot, José Martí, to comment: "What torrents of money! What facilities for every pleasure! The animated groups, the immense dining rooms, the peculiar courtship of North Americans."

Probably the first graffiti outburst in the New World took place in Brooklyn when, on September 14, 1697, a gang of venerable citizens attacked the Kings County Courthouse in Flatbush and defaced the arms of King William of England.

Did you know that Jim Jeffries knocked out Jim Corbett in twenty-three rounds? In Brooklyn.

Did I mention Murder, Inc? Well, they operated out of Brooklyn. We don't hide it; we can't all be churchgoers.

One half of the Brooklyn Bridge was built in Brooklyn. No argument here. And the first man to jump from that Bridge successfully, one Steve Brodie, jumped from the Brooklyn side of the span. His gesture of loyalty.

Where else but in Brooklyn would churches and synagogues hold prayers for Gil Hodges, then first baseman of the Dodgers, to help him break his 1953 batting slump.

Or a famous local poetess Marianne Moore rouse us to baseball glory:

You've got plenty: Jackie Robinson
and Campy and big Newk, and
   Dogerdom again
watching everything you do. You
   won last year. Come on.

Brooklyn has an official flower (forsythia) but no official language. No one I've ever met says "toidy-toid street." But Hart Crane wrote these opening lines to a poem called "The Bridge," which is language enough:

How many dawns, chill from his rippling rest
The seagull's wings shall dip and pivot him,
Shedding white rings of tumult, building high
Over the chained bay waters Liberty—

Back to our opening paragraph: can a place which claims so many illustrious sons and daughters have something in its water, air or character to bring forth such diverse and talented people? Did the aforementioned take character from the place or give character to it? Now we must be careful lest we pile one mystique on top of another.

As a lifelong Brooklyn man myself, I do not know the answer. I have wondered about the answer. But, as a wise man once said, it isn't the answer that's important, but the question. And this particular question, the relation of people to place, is perhaps the most baffling. Cities everywhere boast their share of artists or other celebrities; cities are the hot cauldron, the crucible of human experience; to pick one over another may sound like simple chauvinism.

But if we are an immigrant nation, then Brooklyn is where a high proportion of early Americans settled: it was a quick ferry and trolley ride over from Ellis Island, that famed gateway to the New World. Italian, Jewish, German, Scandinavian—every ethnic and national group —were represented in the vast influx of seekers. A majority of those who brought some fame to Brooklyn came from immigrant backgrounds; their parents were crowded into the tough, restless tenements of Williamsburg, Fort Greene, Red Hook, and the other sections, many of which to this day have retained an ethnic character. These settlers came with dreams along with poverty, and were determined to give their children a chance for a better life. The children, finding opportunity their parents never dreamed of, fought their way up the ladder to vindicate the pride of their parents in the new land. Pride and ambition, and of course talent, were the ingredients that sent these men and women on to fame and sometimes fortune.

Brooklyn was once the bottom for many; it still is to incoming ethnic groups; there is a continuing struggle for space, for survival, for opportunity, among diverse peoples. I contend this mix is part of the creative scene here, part of the turbulence, hope and terror, and optimism, that determines an area, city or borough. Not all of these winners leave. Some stay on, many return, out of nostalgia or to keep the link with parents or relatives from the old country.

Brooklyn may have the quality of outward serenity, but underneath is the tough, open-eyed citizen. Nobody in Brooklyn would ever buy the Brooklyn Bridge, and if he did, he'd open a tollbooth the next morning and cheerfully try to explain things to the police. He might even win.

Walt Whitman exclaimed, in "Crossing Brooklyn Ferry":

> It avails not, time nor place—distance avails not,
> I am with you, you men and women of a generation,
> or ever so many generations hence....

This is still today a place with a sense of continuity, of generations, known to those who were born here, or grew up here, winners or losers. It may not be the nicest place to visit, but I wouldn't want to live anywhere else.

The Curse of the Commercial

"You must do it, you must. Who can we turn to if not our writers and poets? It will only take an hour of your time, and the Committee would be very grateful."

I listened to this eager woman, Janice, and thought, They probably couldn't get the other Norman so they're coming to me, it's been happening a lot lately.

"It would be taping a one-minute commercial," she continued, "though that isn't the correct word exactly—we're not selling anything, we are asking for subscribers that would benefit a worthy cause. Say you'll do it, as a neighborhood gesture." She gave me her brightest smile. Janice was once addicted to the theater as she was now addicted to good works. This particular venture, she explained over the phone before we met, was a magazine set in large type for those with eye diseases and visual difficulties. "You will say on the tape that as a writer you appreciate the value of reading, and those with reading difficulties will receive the same pleasure from this magazine."

"Janice dear," I interrupted gruffly, hoping to move on, "I have enough trouble with my own writing problems, must you burden me with someone else's reading problems?"

"You did promise," she said in her huskiest voice. "You promised over the phone that you'd help. I told them I would be able to get you."

And you have, you vixen, I thought, defeated again by vanity. "Okay, let's do it, you say when, sooner the better. You say a one minute sell, on radio I assume, local use, right?"

"You're a darling," she exclaimed, as she came over to my chair and kissed me on the cheek.

"One minute. May I inquire how many hours to arrange this brief minute?"

She drew a small pad from her purse. "Studio and back, say one hour. Setup should be simple, give it half an hour. Two hours total, and think of the joy this might bring to shut-ins and those with eye difficulties." I nodded, picking at my typewriter keys. "You're hinting that I leave, aren't you?"

"Dear, I am not hinting, I am telling you that I'm at work, and allowed you this interruption—"

"Yes, yes, I'm at fault, I'll leave. In a day or two I'll give you the date of our taping."

"One minute of taping, and I am taping this conversation!"

She laughed, a coquettish laugh fit for a Noël Coward comedy, and left. I had a bad feeling about the future. Outside my window. the Brooklyn sun dropped behind a cloud, as though it were trying to tell me something.

Some weeks later, on a brutally hot day arranged by the gods of mirth, I found myself in a very small recording studio that barely held the equipment and an operator. There, in a small enclosed booth the size of a coffin, reading into a mike, I began, "I'm a writer, and as a writer I also appreciate the pleasures of reading. I know the relaxation that comes with a magazine intelligently prepared for the public. Especially a magazine suitable for those with visual problems. The subscription we are offering is tax deductible—"

A voice piped into the booth interrupted. "Sorry, we screwed up on the voice level. Would you try that again? Take your time, we're testing."

I began again, and was stopped again. "Do you mind, just a bit more pacing, it tends to drag. Thank you. Sorry."

After the first take, Janice squeezed into the booth. "How is it going?"

"Not enough of a sell. After all, we are selling a product."

"Do you think you could fix it? It's less than a page—"

"I am not rewriting. I'm ready to do my fast minute and get the hell out. I've been here over an hour already. This booth is hot. Look, this is hardly a classic, rewrite or no. You've got the basic message, a short pitch, where to send the money, and appreciation, etcetera. Now let's do it. This is not for posterity."

"All right," she replied, seeing my annoyance.

There followed more adjustments for correct volume, a broken tape, and some diction pointers by Janice who thought a poet should show impeccable diction. I never thought much about the spoken word and didn't see why I should worry about it now. Credibility was bound up with speech, Janice explained. After another hour with all the takes, corrections, retakes, a coffee break by the sound man who had a hangover, at last we were finished and I went to the local library to sulk over old *National Geographics*, cursing my neighborhood philanthropic impulse.

Janice had advised me that the "ad" would begin running by week's end on local radio stations, with no set time or station schedule. "It will be everywhere," she crooned. And everywhere it was. Within a week, my voice beamed from every local radio station in the city and its boroughs and adjoining counties. Saturation bombing. At first it amused me to hear myself (vanity, vanity!), but after several weeks I began to dread hearing that inane blurb. It appeared after the stock market report, after a crime survey, before or after every terrorist attack and weather report. I began to avoid these small stations which once gave me pleasure. I tried end-of-the-dial stations, but there I was again, with my nasal drone.

Meanwhile, my friends and the occasional enemy would phone to praise or mock my radio debut. They were delighted that I had got into the money. "What money?" I asked, astounded.

"Come on, kiddo," said Stanley, a fellow writer. "What'd you get, ten, twenty?"

"Twenty what?" I asked.

"Twenty thou, what else? You didn't do it for less, I hope."

"I didn't even get twenty cents. It's not a for-profit organization. Are you mad?"

"You mean you did a freebee?"

"Not even bus fare, I regret to say."

Depression set in. I was approached for loans, for dinner invitations, even a tryst which I didn't follow up in my sour frame of mind. And above it all, morning, noon, and night, my voice floated over the city, calling upon innocent people to subscribe to a magazine I had never seen, if it existed at all. Not even a mess of potage! Not a single piece of silver. Not even Janice!

Well, I thought, I'll shut off my radio for a week, and hide. But neighbors listened, correcting my diction, encouraging me to become an actor, congratulating me (the ugliest implication) that I had got my foot into the money door at last. At first I argued good-naturedly, then I began to snarl and told all callers to leave me alone. This too would pass, I thought. It did not pass; the ad campaign was relentless.

I phoned Janice. "How long is this fucking ad going to run?"

She was shocked at my non-poetic outburst. "People love it," she said.

"I don't care if they love it or eat it for breakfast. How long?"

She hesitated. "I don't know. These ads just fade away . . . finally."

"Well, get it off, will you? I don't like it. My diction is terrible and you coached me."

"Really, Norman, what can I do?"

I hung up, slowly, quietly, tragically. I was trapped, caught in the jaws of technology. Low man in a high-tech world. I called my agent. I did not have to explain the situation—she and everyone in the office had heard that commercial.

"It keeps your name before the public," she reasoned.

"I want you to help me get that off the air. It does not suit my character."

"This isn't a question of character," she replied with a careless laugh. "Look at it as free advertising. It doesn't matter what is being said. Your name is associated with a product, which can mean, in the subliminal mind, that you are *somebody!*"

"Do you know what Emily Dickinson wrote? 'I'm nobody. Who are you?/ How dreary to be somebody.' Emily wrote that," I yelled.

"You mustn't worry so much about these silly things. Sit down and write a best seller. Goodbye for now."

I left the house and walked along the Promenade, brooding, planning my revenge . . . but how? Even the sight of my beloved Bridge did not lift my spirits. An approaching dog walker turned out to be the other Norman.

"Don't you know," I began belligerently, "it's against the law to walk your dog on the Promenade?"

"Yeah, but city people like to sidestep shit." He grinned. "Anyway, breaking the law is an urban necessity."

"What's that smudge near your eye?"

"It shows, heh? I could say I ran into a doorknob, but how can I lie before the poet laureate? A critic lady took a swipe at me and didn't miss." He chuckled. "I tell you, kid, the last frontier isn't space, it's women, and that should keep the writers busy for centuries, or until sex is passé which it is now almost."

"What's replacing it?"

"That's easy. Food." He glanced at his watch. "I'd better get back. How's with you?"

"I've got a problem. I'd like to kill someone."

"That's what your agent is for."

"I asked her but she refused."

"My man Scott would do it for a client. Never too late to switch." The dog barked. "Come on, you little fucker." He patted the dog and they left in a light trot.

I waited for my barrister at the tennis club of which I am not now nor have ever been a member, being of the more primitive handball breed (gloves as well as paddle). He emerged with that look of power I dislike in athletes, clearly the look of a winner.

"Lawrence. Have we time for coffee?"

"Not even a quick one served by a topless waitress," he said with a smile not of a lawyer but of a decent citizen. "Since I never bill you for advice, let's have it out on the street, high noon, hey?" Lawrence was my dollar-a-year lawyer as befitted a dollar-a-year laureate. (Actually we had a barter arrangement, his advice exchanged for a stray erotic lyric.)

"I'm trying to get out of something and—"

"You're guilty," he yodeled. He won his match, he was high. "If you knocked her up, you gotta pay."

"Larry, can I revoke an oral agreement, sort of?"

"I don't like the sound of it, but what is it?"

I began to explain, but he soon cut in. "Did you sign a paper, a contract of any sort? I won't ask if there was money involved, I smell the answer. Did they give you anything to indicate your rights?"

"Rights to what?"

"To that cockamamie script, such as who owns it, how often they can use it, termination, etc. Nothing like that, right? You just did a good civic deed. So now go home, boychick, and write a best seller like *Crime and Punishment*, which would make a good mini-series. There's nothing else you can do."

"I can't force them to stop?"

"Legally, you have no rights, it's poetic justice, ha ha. I heard that thing, the kids love to hear your voice, Kathy too. Got to rush. Come by tonight for some spaghetti. Ciao!"

Can I trust my neighbors, friends, defrocked lawyers or account executives, assorted roamers of the Brooklyn steppes? I phoned the studio where I had recorded the commercial. The manager said he had no authority beyond making the tape for reproduction purposes; all distribution and other details were the responsibility of the owners of the tape, whoever they were. Like a maddened urban victim, I decided to make a final plea for justice. I called Janice, dear earnest Janice.

"Are you going to shout at me?" she began severely.

"Not today. One question. Can you kindly tell me who owns the tape, or who has distributed it in how many million copies?"

"I sincerely don't know. I worked through a contact of the magazine. I can give you the phone number."

"That would be decent of you, Janice."

"There's no need to be angry. That commercial is being well received. Maybe it has even enhanced your reputation—"

With a muted howl, I cut her off. Almost sensing the next scene in this psychodrama, I dialed the number. A click, then a voice on tape: "*The number you have dialed—226-8804—has been disconnected.*" End of the trail. Technology had cunningly covered its tracks.

The commercial, like a wandering space signal, faded after several months of insane repetition. I would hear it dimly, and wonder whose voice was doing such a good British imitation. I couldn't be bothered with it any longer. I was too busy writing a best seller, convinced that corruption brings out the deepest talent in people.

A Street Car Named Falcon

One day I went out to look for my street car. It's twelve years old, with fading paint, telltale signs of body rust, and a sad, neglected appearance. A street car is a particularly sturdy kind of vehicle, immune to climate and most bacteria; it survives unsheltered unlike its delicate cousin, the garaged car.

Such car, furthermore, needs a careful owner or it risks being misplaced; it is a car parked on so many streets that one can often lose track of it. I have always feared such a memory loss. The thought of my Falcon, abandoned, laden with undeserved parking tickets, abused by dogs or mischievous children, is too much to bear. I am careful to make a sharp mental note where it is after I park.

I find it on this day, forlorn and unwashed (no rain for several weeks), a far cry from our first meeting, its speedometer then barely at 3000 miles. I wasn't sure about this particular car, but an honest relative wanted to unload it at a fair price. Here it is, into its second decade and some 80,000 miles later. My friends have each been through three cars on the average while I have that same Falcon. I turn the key: instant response. Smooth getaway. Who needs a Rolls or Cadillac? The laureate looks and laughs at all that.

A few months ago it appeared the Falcon and I had come to a parting of the ways. A tow truck swooped down and ... well, you know the story. I journeyed to the car pound where I faced on $85-retrieval fee. Eighty-five! The market value wasn't much higher. I hurried to where the car was parked along the piers. Should I take one last look and walk away? It seemed a perfectly reasonable ending to a long friendship. I looked at this honorable street car, heavy with urban film, bruised and dented, sagging slightly on weakened springs. It was metal and glass, but at this moment I felt it had a soul. Thoughts of those years of reliability raced through my mind.

I particularly recalled one evening in winter, around midnight, in a long-term parking lot at Kennedy Airport. I had just arrived on a flight from Denver after a holiday of ecstatic skiing and, skis on my shoulder, alighted from the airport bus in this deserted area. There had been a storm and the lot was covered with deep snow. I trudged against a sharp wind to where my Falcon waited, half-hidden in a drift. It was about ten degrees above zero. A white moon floated overhead, good for poets but bad for anyone about to start a car that had been standing idle for a week and looked frozen. Skis and equipment inside, I sat behind the wheel and inserted the ignition key. It was a moment of truth. I said aloud, fervently, "Baby, we're miles from a garage, I can't hail a cab. You're cold, I'm cold, your sparkplugs are coated with ice, not to mention oil at the firing gaps, but I beg you to start. If you start, I'll buy you new brakes and tires. I'll love and cherish you. Just don't fail me now!"

I turned the key. The Falcon groaned, coughed once—and victory! I wouldn't say I wept with emotion, but if I could have stretched my arms around this metal shape, I would have hugged her/him/it. The motor hummed, and I remember shouting in the cold, "I'll never leave you!" Not only snowy nights of triumph, but rainy mornings as well. How often a neighbor would show up with an embarrassed grin and say "I can't start my new Volvo and I'm late for work. Can I borrow your heap? It always starts in the rain."

Such words are a comfort, yet at that moment in the car pound I realized that my Falcon, sturdy in spirit, was at a ripe old age. Well, I was not going to leave that body and spirit there. Painfully, I wrote out the required check. The car was mine again. Ignition on. Reprieved! Could it be, as I drove off . . . the sound of galloping hooves in the air? Falcon away!

The life and destiny of my car is inextricably bound up with Melvin, my garage man. He not only keeps it in minimal repair (certain things remain unrepairable) but officially inspects it every year. He has the awesome power to keep it off the streets and possibly—if repairs are too high—to condemn it to death. When I'd show up for my annual inspection, he'd greet me with mock derision. "Well, looka here, don't tell me it's that old spaceship again. You mean she's lasted another whole year?" He'd grin sardonically to imply it might not pass inspection this time. But on picking it up later, there was the usual new sticker on the windshield. "One thing for sure," he'd say, each year, shaking his head, "you won't be bringing in that relic next year." I'd start the motor, and reply, "Would you care to bet on it?"

Mel was a cheerful fellow generally, but he could be irascible. He particularly enjoyed picking on my old Falcon. "God would be good to you if He let your car get stolen."

"You're sore because I don't garage it in your high-price emporium."

"The germs on your car, kid, would kill a Mercedes."

I had to laugh at that. "How come a nice guy like you has all that hostility?"

"I don't know, I try to be lovable. So why don't you break down and get a new car? The other Norman has a Citroën, classy job, you can tilt it, must be great for the ladies." He rubbed his unshaven jaw.

"By the way, Mel—"

"Another complaint, I see it comin'. You passed the inspection, didn't you?"

"Sure, but you overcharged me. I didn't need that new radiator hose, it wasn't cracked like it says on the bill."

He closed his eyes for a moment. "Last year was the same thing, you accused me about the sparkplugs. Now it's the new radiator hose. You saw the old one, I left it on the car seat."

"It was maybe beginning to crack, but it had a year to go, at least. You're just conning the motorist."

He shook his head wearily. "Listen, your hose breaks while you're driving over the bridge and where are you? Up shit creek, tow job, the works. So you ought to thank me for spotting that hose and replacing it."

"Eighteen bucks."

"Come by later, I'll turn back five."

"It's the principle, Mel. The consumer has to fight back."

"Hey, we won't argue about a lousy eighteen bucks. Did I tell you I took your book out of the library?"

"So what'd you think?"

"Okay." He winked. "But like the hose, y'know, cracked." He guffawed, slapped me on the shoulder, and hustled off.

Late Bloomer

He first approached me coming out of the subway station, my eyes blinking in the sharp afternoon light so that I did not notice him until he was at my side.

"Howdy," he said in a boyish cheerful voice, his face open and smiling, like one of the Seven Dwarfs. "Nice to see you."

I nodded. His face looked familiar, I had seen him before, I recalled, at the same subway entrance. He was a smallish man, on the elderly side but with energy in his speech and stride that had the stamp of youth.

He continued, "I've been meaning a number of times . . . I see you a lot in the neighborhood, never got up the courage." He hesitated. "I hope you won't take it amiss, but I'm a writer, at least I hope I am, and to come right out with it, would you be able possibly to look at some of my work? Poetry, that is, if that's what it is."

He saw the tremor of my hesitation, and plunged ahead. "There isn't much to show, and you being the poet laureate . . . "

That last almost turned me off. Still, he was polite, well dressed, and I figured better to go through the unknown than try to avoid it. "Tell you what—"

"Meredith is my name."

"Okay, now you haven't got a six-hundred-and eighty-page narrative poem about the Crusades or something like that."

"No, sir. Just maybe thirty short pieces, poems, but there are days when I'm not sure, and your opinion would be much appreciated."

The man was sincere, which didn't mean I had to fall for it, but I did.

He was definitely not buttering me up. He had a problem, and wasn't I the dollar-a-year fixer?

"Meredith," I said, as we began walking down Henry Street, "If you drop them off at my house, drop them and leave, I'll have a look. You're not to phone me the next day or week and ask if I've read them."

"Oh, I wouldn't do that."

"Or when I tell you what I think, you don't call me a liar."

He laughed. "I wouldn't dream of doing that. I never asked this kind of favor before, you see." We walked for a moment in silence, then he said, "I'd be happy to pay you for your time."

"No, that's out. I hope I like the poems. Time, by the way, is not money. It's a form of space, if you know your Einstein."

"I haven't given it much thought," Meredith said. "I don't write much, and I've been quiet about it, but lately I've been wondering."

I liked his free-floating speech. It would be sad if he couldn't write a line. As we approached the corner where the fates reside, he said, "I'm turning off here. I'll drop my work by in a few days, leave it at your door and scoot." With a swift little nod, he walked off.

Several days later, my buzzer sounded. A voice on the intercom announced, "It's Meredith. I'll leave my envelope in the lobby, don't want to interrupt. Thank you." It clicked out. So far, he was a gentleman. I was in no hurry to get to his envelope, with my disappointing experience in unsolicited manuscripts. One night I shortened my bedtime Montaigne to try a bit of Meredith and see if it would put me to sleep. It didn't. The first page, while no masterpiece, had the unmistakable flow and crackle of life. "Hotel Room Saturday Night" was the title.

> The wall
> was a roadmap of sounds.
> They ran around
> moaning and groaning
> and made love somewhere
> between Scranton and Saskatchewan.
> My mind jumped
> the track,

took after you
with flying colors,
bought you a box
of arm-length gloves
to wear,
and nothing else.

I read the other thirty or so small-sized lyrics and thought whatever this guy has or has not, I could honestly say he was a poet. A late bloomer. The next day I phoned to tell him so and ask him to drop by.

He did, smiling and astonished that I had not only read his stuff, but had good things to say about it. "With the power vested in me by the borough president," I intoned, "I officially proclaim you a poet. May the gods be kind to you, for editors will not." He almost danced with glee.

We chatted in the kitchen over coffee. I suggested he check some of his punctuation eccentricities, such as lots of dashes, and also noted his strange use of the comma which in some instances would perplex the reader.

"For example, what's this comma doing here, with another single word on the next line hanging out to dry. It doesn't look right."

He nodded. "I do that for my reading."

"To whom?"

"To friends. I'm a ham, I read with gestures and voice, and my peculiar commas and dashes help me get the right effect."

"Meredith, since you're a poet emerging from the cave, so to speak, my advice is to forget about oral effect. Let the words themselves give the effect, and the music they resonate. See your work on the page. Punctuate for your readers to help get the meaning. Declamation is okay for your own bathroom, but poetry isn't show business. This said, forget everything I said, punctuate as you damn please."

"Well, I appreciate your advice."

"Take it only if you're comfortable with it. You're in charge, remember."

We were both pleased when we marked the same poems as favorites. Our easy exchange took an hour and gave him the confidence he needed; for myself, it was simply the fun of talking about poetry. I suggested he try some of the little magazines, and maybe a big one like The New Yorker just for the hell of it. That name almost blew him away.

"Why not?" I said. "Just be prepared to get them back. See it as a game whose delight is in the playing, and where you show your hand. Enjoy it!"

As he got up to leave, Meredith pushed an envelope across the table. "This is for you. It's just a small token."

"No, please, I couldn't. I told you—"

"I insist. I'd feel bad if you refused. I took up your time, and suppose you were a doctor or lawyer, wouldn't it be right to pay a fee? I'm not wealthy, and this isn't much . . . I'd feel better. Go on, take it, please."

I didn't know how to refuse, though I resolutely wished to. I sensed he didn't want to "owe" me anything, being a new acquaintance. He was asking me not to embarrass him.

"Okay, Meredith. Since you insist, and I'm easygoing, I'll take it."

"Thank you."

"Actually, I didn't do much, but then what the hell does a doctor do for his fee?"

"At least your work is honest," he laughed. "You've done something very important for me, though you may not know it. You've excited me about my work, its possibilities. I'll take your advice, mail some stuff out and see what happens."

"I hope something does, even a small thing."

He set his cap at a jaunty angle. "Even if they all come back, something good has happened already, do you see?" He held out his hand. "I hope we meet again, maybe on the street." We shook hands.

"Let me know if you place anything. One lyric would be enough. Lyrics are what's holding the world together, not gravity or ions or rubber cement."

"Couldn't agree more." He grinned as I led him to the door. Again, that quick nod, and he was gone.

I opened the envelope. Two tens and a five. I really didn't want it, but understood his need to offer it and for me to accept. Yet I had to find a way to satisfy my own feelings. I called him that same evening. I said I enjoyed his visit but would take that doctor's fee only on the condition that he allow me to send him one or two of my own books in exchange. He said he'd be delighted. I suggested my *Selected Poems* for one. And perhaps a novel.

"Let me borrow the novel," he said.

"Meredith, this time I shall insist. You will not borrow, but take both, and spread the song of iambic pentameter, or any other tune, across the land. Is that a deal?"

"A deal."

To show he was serious, Meredith mailed this little reminder days later.

> Sunlight makes a plaque
> out of every wavering leaf,
> prints on it accolades
> for a job well done.
> There are calls for "Speech! Speech!"
> to which the leaves finally acquiesce,
> and talk . . . and talk . . . and
> talk!

Soon after I heard a shout from across the street. It was he. He grinned and waved. I waved. Then I to my Xerox, he to his poems. And I suppose God to his world.

Corners

There's Broadway and Forty-second Street, Hollywood and Vine; and in Brooklyn Heights Montague and Henry—to name just a few famous corners. For the latter, I suspect part of its popularity is due to the three phones and a railing to lean against while friend or foe wanders by. People going about their business need a corner to pause and reflect.

I'm sure there are other popular corners where people gather; for some reason, which could possibly be explained sociologically, the middle of the block is not a good gathering point. Do humans, like migrating birds, return to the same corners day after day or year? What attracts them?

Montague and Henry has the newspaper kiosk, an advantage for any corner. Police Officer O'Neil is often found here, looking grim or smiling, depending on whether anyone's paying attention. O'Neil belongs on this corner; he adds to its respectability. (By the way, haven't seen hime lately, hope he's well.) My personal mailman Tommy Fischetti often pauses here on his daily rounds, and Tommy is always good for an idle piece of history. Once when asked, "What was your biggest mail delilvery?" he responded without pausing, "A $25,000 check in a registered letter. And I can tell you, I was glad to get that check out of my bag." I told Tommy about my own recent $300 check for royalties in Finland or some such exotic place, but he was only mildly interested. A man who once delivered a $25,000 check won't get fired up by much under $5,000.

Charming and unimportant people gather at the corner. You'd like Walter. He's my favorite corner-lounger, a man of elegance and sensibility, an ex-Austrian nobleman of sorts who has tales of earlier pristine days on Montague. The corner is a good place for eavesdropping, if you go in for such sport. Brief and mysterious fragments of conversation drift from the open phone booths (open eavesdropping). I hear an impassioned, "'Send the money,' I told him. So I'm waiting for the check. He gets nothing until I get the check!" I hear, "Meet you anywhere, baby. You name it. You got a friend? Bring your friend..." Two young women hurry by, leave a sentence trailing behind them like perfume: "I only just met the man, and when he asked me, I refused...." Asked what? Refused what? Maybe the next corner has the answers.

Street encounters (corners or not) are the grist of the day. You're never sure who's going to interrupt to test your stamina or sanity. For example, a neighbor wants my opinion: should he allow animals—dogs, cats, canaries, even the child's pet hamster—into the room while human sex is under way? Not just in the room, but often on the bed or, if a bird, perched with a winking eye on a lamp or bedpost. What's to be done if dear little terrier wants to sit there quietly and watch? Or watch and howl? Can the furry fellow tell an erection from a rubber bone? My opinion may be worthless but it is sincere. Opinions are exchanged on gardening, poetry, the other Norman (a favorite topic) and nuclear annihilation. The outdoors frees the spirit for confessionals. Thus neighbors reveal what often deserves to be hidden, such as the latest adultery, who's the new alcoholic on the block, who is impotent, or which teenager is misbehaving in the back of the family stationwagon.

Corners are great places for complainers. If you stand there long enough, or often enough, you take on a sort of official presence, and pretty soon people are complaining to you about dogs, police brutality, parking problems, filthy streets, sexual molestation in the St. George lobby, the CIA, blacks. Not much about air pollution or political corruption or government lying; that's too obvious, I guess. There are, of course, those suspicious of all corner dwellers. Watch out for them!

Is the corner of Montague and Clinton more appealing than Montague and Henry? Or, to put it another way, is an ice-cream store at Henry outclassed by a church and bank at Clinton?

I admit to an emotional preference for the Clinton corner, for its two institutions are dear to my heart. I was married in one, and am a depositor at the other. I did some writing many years ago in both these edifices, in rooms normally reserved for prayer and bullion. I'm not sure which setting had a greater influence in my work: I'm as far from heaven as ever, and my back account does not overimpress.

Banks often look like churches on the inside; in fact, they can give off a churchly glow quite akin to religious feeling—at least, Manufacturers Hanover (opposite St. Ann's) has that air with its spaciousness and marble decoration. I could as well be inside a Venetian Church. Height is the first seductive detail; the vaulted ceiling somehow seems fitting for both money and holiness, the hush reflects the sanctity of money gathering interest even while we mortals sleep. And is not money the dominant American religion? Profit and piety make good scripture.

Lucky the Brooklyn Union Gas Company! By being in the middle of the block it will escape my scrutiny—though I do not forget the lost library that once occupied the same space.* Its dear ghost whispers as I pass, "Do not forget me," and I will not, for I was there when they demolished that fine old nineteenth-century building. Nor do I forget the lost footbridge over the then descending Montague Street leading below to Furman, before the era of the Promenade; nor Walt Whitman's printing shop once at Fulton and Cranberry, the tennis courts that stood at Remsen & Henry, the park at Montague and Montague Terrace —such sights once graced the corners of Brooklyn Heights.

---

*My new library, air-conditioned,
scientifically lighted, I'm sure the place
is germ-proof—why am I unhappy here?
The old library (two blocks away,
erected 1886 and recently torn down
for the new Gas building) was my first love.
I knew its gothic doors and timber,
the open rotunda and creaking floors;
the radiators knocked, pigeons stared in,
dogs and derelicts often entered
along with scholars: it all made sense.
And where's the old drunk dozing
under Lincoln's head?—back to the gutter.

Progress erodes the corners first, which brings us back to Montague and Clinton. No escape. Between church and bank our destiny hovers. Keep a small account in each, friend, for you'll nver know which is the lasting currency until you're about to go down for the third time.

The other day while hunting for my parked car I passed the corner of Pierrepont and Hicks and thought of my friend, the elegant writer Ira Wallach, who lived for a time on this very corner. Departed, alas. He didn't die, he moved away, and I wondered how this ex-Brooklynite was faring since he left the holy sod. Another of Mr. Wallach's corner residences (surely a sign of the elite) was Clinton and State, where he lived with a wife, child, and one-eyed addle-brained dog who laughed at his funny lines. There he wrote some of his books and plays, including the famous Hopalong Freud, the should-have-been famous Gutenberg's Folly and almost famous Broadway play, Absence of a Cello. But enough, let his agent do his PR work.

Then, mysteriously, he emigrated to Manhattan in search of a better life and greater royalties—and where did he settle? On another corner: Fifty-eighth and Ninth! (A psychiatrist could fool around with this.) It is too late to call out, "Come back, Ira, all is forgiven!" Once they leave, they rarely return. Those who cross the Brooklyn Bridge in wrath, lament in sorrow. Ira found a new wife and has a snappy new Manhattan-style typewriter that runs on wind-generated current. Arthur Miller should never have left, he lost his Brooklyn roots and became

---

In short, another crime has been committed
in the name of Progress and I protest.
May the Gas Company be haunted forever
by Whitman and Stendhal, and may Marlowe
the hothead roaming those deep cellars
set off (accidentally) the sirens
to waken the city and the sleeping mayor.

This will bring my grievance to light,
the forgotten voice of my murdered library.

rootless. The other Norman was wise enough, when shipwrecked, to swim back to shore.

I phoned Ira some time ago; he sleeps late and loves to be disturbed. He had not been out of bed for days.

"Are you happy on your new corner, Ira?"

"Yes. Happy as a mouse on a cheesehill."

"Don't you miss the old corner of Pierrepont and Hicks?"

"No. All corners are basically the same, allowing you to turn. Hence the expression, the country has turned a corner."

"Why don't we meet downtown for lunch and gossip, and attack famous authors like we used to do?"

"Goody. What about a week from today. Same time."

"Where?"

"Let's say Eighth and University? See you then."

Still the true Corner Man!

Almost any street corner has potential to be the scene of a crime, so when I pick on Hicks and Clark I don't mean to neglect the others. It just happens that I know someone who was unhappily on H & C when lightning struck. Luckily, this friend ran into a rather decent fellow who didn't brandish a knife or threaten undue violence. Merely a grim voice that urged a transference of cash without delay, to which my friend complied. This transaction swiftly accomplished, the mugger parted from the muggee; no bloodshed, but enough of a scare to trouble my friend's sleep for a month.

I have known others who have been mugged, or had a purse snatched, or been stripped of a watch. But, as in matters of rape, I'm certain most of the assaults are either unreported or simply untold. Recent statistics seem to show that these criminal acts are on the downgrade. Could it be that the mugger, like any good American, is looking elsewhere for a larger income? Are car thefts rising? Or simple larceny? The mugger likes to distribute wealth, which is not quite the same thing as creating it.

This subject is no laughing matter to those who have experienced it head-on. Yet we know that the human race often faces adversity with humor, which brings me to a neighborhood survey I've conducted on how people think other people should act to avoid a mugger. To begin with, don't look muggable—a small but vital point. Those who dawdle, walk hesitantly, appear to be lost or confused (a common urban feeling), often invite attack by their seeming weakness. Look confident, even aggressive. I know of a neighbor who practices looking like a karate champ and a policewoman; she scowls, hunches her shoulders as she walks, and has developed an icy stare. She tried it out on me; I trembled with apprehension last we pass on a dark street and she misinterpreted my friendly greeting.

There are those who feel the best defense is to confound the intended attacker by psychological means. For example, one imaginative night roamer has developed a limp which he uses when approaching a "dangerous" looking person, the theory being that a criminal would not attack one who is handicapped (wanna bet?). Another, coming out of the St. George subway at midnight, hits the street talking to himself, a rambling monologue, occasionally swinging his arms, hoping to put a scare into the potential attacker: don't fool with a crazy man. (The danger is that this man might absently enter his own apartment still doing his act and meeting his wife in the hallway or bedroom.) I'm not sure feigned madness is the answer; we have too many of the truly mad to contend with.

Meanwhile, I'm busy practicing my own survival technique. Should you spot a figure with handball gloves or paddle on some dark night moving along Willow or Sidney Place (great streets for mischief), it might be me. Don't approach, you might get clobbered.

Personals

"Are you having an affair with my wife?" David asked jovially on a Tuesday morning at the corner of Montague and Hicks.

"No. Scout's honor," I replied. And it is known that I am an honorable man.

He thought for a moment. "If an affair can spark up a dull marriage, that's good. But one may get to like it, that's bad." He sighed. "You see all around you old marriages suddenly blossom, that's when to be alert, there's a neighbor in the chicken coop."

"Do you think your wife is having an affair?" (It was as good a subject as any while waiting for the lights to change.)

"No. But it's the kind of gloomy day when anything seems possible."

Not to be outdone by this philosophic thrust, I said, "It's the possible that gives beauty to all things, David. That's how it is with painting, as I don't have to tell a great artist like yourself. If not greatness, the possiblity . . . " He smiled faintly at this. "As with writing a poem. I would say possibility is the critical element, having to do with the weight of the word, the balance of the line, whether it can be done, and you try. Over the falls!"

He nodded solemnly. "So we're back to sex."

"Do you know the *Grosse Fugue?*"

"Is that Bach?"

"Ludwig von B, who will illustrate my theory of possibility. Since we're on the subject, if you had one hour to live, what would you choose to do? Wrong. After sex you have what the French call *la tristesse,* the ultimate post-coital sadness which means you'll go to your grave depressed. But if you listened instead to the *Grosse Fugue* with its incredible pattern, possibility triumphant, you would depart the world in a state of exhilaration, beatitude, and peace."

"I enjoyed your speech. Let me think about it." He glanced at his watch.

"Where are you off to?" I asked. "You look worried."

"I should be. I'm going to Staten Island."

"Why are you going to that forsaken outpost, David?"

He stared into space. "Frankly, I'm not sure. You see before you a man working the Coney Island beaches for twenty years, mostly watercolors, and I have the bad luck to meet a fellow who suggests I try another island for material. It's the way he put it. He said, 'Have you ever seen the Other Side of Staten Island?' I thought it was only the Other Side of the moon that existed. The dark side. Can it be there's a dark side to Staten Island, with beaches and Jewish people? Why not? After half a lifetime in Coney, why not Staten? I may find mermaids there, even a germ-free beach, who knows?"

The lights changed, and we crossed over.

"Is this goodbye, then?"

"With luck, I'll be back on a late ferry." He took a step, then turned. "Have you done anything on that Personals idea? If you've forgotten, let me remind you that I'm waiting for you to write some wild titbits for a fake Personals column. I'll do the drawings. We'll make some Christmas or Passover money. Now get on it, or I'll ask the other Norman." He hurried toward the subway, good neighborhood man, bless him.

Taking his threat seriously, I hurried to the Promenade, found an empty bench and, opening my small notebook, sketched out some Personals. I was determined to deliver them that same day.

> Male mountain climber, middle-aged, virile, wishes
> compassionate relationship with erotic spinster,
> age unimportant if she can yodel.

> Non-political Arab studying for his doctorate in
> New York, handsome, lonely, wants to meet broadminded
> and sexually inclined Jewess.

One-legged skier, charming, great lover (2 arms),
seeks optimistic soulmate who enjoys reading the
novels of Jane Austen aloud as après-ski pleasure.

Young virgin, wild, enjoys camping and outdoors, in
love with life and the wilderness, seeking reformed
drug addict to deflower her in Yellowstone National park.

Handball player, 30, hardhat type, interested in
ballet, searching for female companion to complete
group for 4-wall tournament. Gloves and black ball,
no paddles. Sex optional.

Society woman, 50, gracious hostess, dog lover,
attempting to mate her female terrier with gentle male
of same species, at the same time indulging in sex
herself. Communication in strictest confidence.

Had it with Women's Lib? If you want an old-fashioned
face-to-face bang-bang lover, a macho anthropologist
doing field work with the Hopi Indians, send photo
and closeup of breasts front and side view. Yumyum.
Fun guaranteed.

As I was racing along, I felt the presence of someone seated next to
me on the bench. "Am I interrupting any important creative work?" a
voice asked. "If so, I promise to be quiet."

It was Doris, a rather plain, shy, young middle-aged widow who had
hinted a number of times that she would welcome male attention—not
from me, she hastened to add, but anyone I might know in the state of
widowhood or divorce. "I should be sitting next to an eligible bachelor
right now," she said, "if I knew how to spot one."

"Or a married man," I added dryly. I liked Doris (she liked my books)
and we got into small talk about the difficulties of meeting people in
big cities. Then she startled me by saying she had been reading some
Personals columns and thought she might try her hand at composing
one for herself.

"That's a good idea," I replied, "and very much in vogue."

"You don't think it's foolish, do you, a woman going through this sort
of thing," she said, embarrassed, her voice low.

"Not at all. Why is it foolish?"

"It's like doing a striptease, don't you think?"

"I don't. And even if it were, Doris, you're stripping for a good cause."

She smiled shyly. "What's the cause?"

"A man."

She sighed. "I'd never thought I'd stoop to this."

"It's not stooping. It's an act of courage. You're reaching out for something, and I admire that."

"It could only be more trouble." Then, she looked at me and with a burst of childish candor, at the moment very endearing. She said, "Wouldn't it be nice if you and I were in love instead of just friends?" Topped with a little laugh.

I reached over and patted her hand. "Friends are reserved for the best people," I said. "Now, about that Personals ad, what are you planning to say?"

She hesitated. What I dreaded would come, came. "I thought I would ask you to write it, you being the writer."

I tried to recover. "You can do it. You don't have to be a writer. Just think about what it is you want to say about yourself to attract a man. And say it."

"You say it for me. Whatever you think. I'd appreciate it." Now she smiled almost seductively, and I thought with a bit of luck she should be able to make some man happy. But where to find him? Was it in a Personals column? I felt he was somewhere closer, perhaps the next street.

"Tell you what, Doris, I'll sketch something out and read it to you over the phone. After all, it needn't be more than a few sentences. Well turned, of course."

Her eyes brightened. "Make it a little sexy because from what I read in those columns you need that or you're dead."

"Not true," I replied. "Sex is a sell, sure, but the real sell is character. Our job is to catch your character in a few deathless sentences."

"I'm sure you can do it."

"You do, eh? I'll try."

"I'll be glad to pay you."

"My dollar-a-year appointment will cover it," and this time I laughed. Dimly I saw my fate entwined with the fates of others.

I phoned Doris several days later and read her the following: "Young middle-aged woman, intelligent, warm-spirited. Wishes to love the right man who has a heart to match mine. Sex can easily blossom, as well as laughter. No photographs but tender words welcomed."

I waited. There was silence, audible, electric, an unheard ticking clock. Then her voice, "It's beautiful. Is that me? Is that how you see me?"

"It's how we want others to see you. I do think it says a lot about you, as I've known you as friend and neighbor."

She repeated slowly, "Is that how you see me?"

"Yes, but that's not the point." We were moving into choppy waters, and, I sensed, beyond my volunteer duties as laureate. I had no intention of becoming Dear Abby.

"Let me think about it," she said.

"Whatever you wish. And if you want anything added, or subtracted ..." I laughed. "Some rewrite allowed, but not too much."

"You're very kind. I like it, really. But ..."

"Take your time, give me a call later in the week."

My wife, who generally stayed out of these literary games, commented, when asked, "She's a sweet person, but you're rushing in where angels fear to tread."

What a line, wish I had written it!

She continued. "If Doris gets a man through that ad, and it turns out badly, you're the villain, remember that."

"I always remember what you tell me—too late."

"Though I suspect it's you she wants, darling."

"Me? She wouldn't dare try to steal me away from you. Or would she? And what do I do?"

"You go or you stay. Look how simple I make it for you."

I didn't like her reply exactly, or the faint smile on her face. "May I read you what I wrote for her Personals ad?"

"No," she replied briskly, and sent me shopping.

While browsing in the Cereal-Pancake aisle, I met Doris. She seemed embarrassed, and stopped for a moment. "I meant to call you," she said, "I'm not too sure that was the right tone for the ad. It sounds too ... inviting, too sensual."

"Well, isn't that what we want? You hope to invite someone, it's the name of the game, isn't that so?"

She turned away. "I'm not happy with it. I'm sorry to have bothered you. It just doesn't seem right."

"I think it's a good ad. But it's your decision."

"Yes, I know. Thank you." She pressed my hand and moved on to Meat-Fish. I sauntered over to Fruit-Vegetables, my favorite browsing section.

Weeks passed, perhaps a month. I ran into Doris on the pedestrian ramp of the Brooklyn Bridge. She was pale and appeared under stress; we smiled and stopped awkwardly in the way of conspirators. She took a step as if to pass me, hesitated, and said, "I thought you'd call me about . . . the problem."

"I assumed you'd given up on it."

She moved to the side to let the joggers go by. "Yes, maybe I have. But I've been having a rough time. I can't take it much longer, the way I'm living, the loneliness . . ."

"I'm sorry to hear that."

"I don't think you want to help me." The words were out of her mouth effortlessly, but her eyes narrowed with malevolence. "You save all the good words for your stories, and when I ask for help, you offer me some old worn-out words. If you want to know the truth—"

"Wait a minute," I interrupted, startled by her vehemence, her bitterness. "Those words were chosen for your particular situation. What else did you expect me to do?"

"Why couldn't you write something to really get me a man, to make someone want me? You're a writer, why couldn't you?" Now her voice rose, she was oblivious to the heads turning to observe us as they passed by. "If you can't help me, what's the point? Write something about me that *you* believe, that you honestly see in me. Can you do that?" Her intensity shook and disturbed me.

"I'm sorry, Doris. What more can I do?"

She seized my arm. "You can love me."

"I can't. I love my wife."

"She wouldn't know."

"It's too difficult, the whole thing."

She turned to go. "Let's forget the ad. It's all too late, don't you understand? You made a fool of me for encouraging me to go ahead with this. It's a lie, you knew it, you wouldn't tell me." She dashed off.

I remained there, staring into space, into the webbing of the Bridge. Where angels fear to tread! I felt unable to rise to the occasion, whatever that was. A cyclist raced by, almost knocking me over as I jumped out of his path. I shouted after him, "Damn fool idiot, I hope you crash through the rail into the water!"

Coming off the ramp, as I waited for the light to change, it began to rain. A car braked to a halt at the curb. A head leaned out of the window. It was the Boro Prez, collar open, tie loosened, the look of a sportsman. "How's it going with the poet laureate?" he called out cheerfully.

"Not my best day, Howie."

"At least you have time for a nap. Drop by the office, I'll tell you some of *my* problems. Ciao!" He waved, rolled up the window, and drove away.

Marilyn

Sweetly remembered, Marilyn Monroe came to Brooklyn one day to shoot publicity photos in Prospect Park with photographer Sam Shaw. That same afternoon, escaping the rain, they both found refuge at my house. He had phoned and asked if it was okay to bring his model. I recall she came up the stairs behind Sam, hesitant, wearing an oversized camel's hair coat, no makeup, hair short and careless and wet. I watched from above as she turned onto the second floor of the curving stairwell. She looked from that point like any pretty high school kid. Sam was an old friend of mine, a professional photographer on an assignment, I assumed, with this woman model.

He introduced her casually, he mumbled her name and it sounded like Marion. I still recall her shy, "Pleased to meet you." She found a chair in the living room where she sat rather stiffly, her eyes mischievous and warm. She snuggled into the chair with a shy smile. I noticed her shoes were wet and suggested she remove them. She did. My wife entered to say hello and immediately went out to put up some coffee. Then we chatted, small talk about the weather and Brooklyn, this being her first visit to our fabled kingdom. She listened more than she spoke; her sentences were short, breathless. Soon my wife returned with coffee, cake, and dry stockings. The rain continued outside. My wife politely inquired as to our visitor's profession. Was she an actress?

"No," she replied, "I've never been on the stage. But I have done some movies."

"What was your last one? And what was your movie name?"

In a timid voice: "Marilyn Monroe."

Sam heard this and laughed. "Didn't I tell you? I guess I didn't get around to it. It's her, all right."

It was the famous "her" without a doubt. And our first meeting did not end there. That same evening we invited them both to come along to a party in the neighborhood, at the Schumans. Marilyn laughed when I said nobody would recognize her the way she was dressed; the thought didn't bother her at all. And so, a few hours later, we walked the three blocks to the party. I introduced her with, "I'd like you to meet a friend, Marilyn Monroe." Nobody believed me. They continued to drink and talk, accepting the joke (they thought) in good spirit. Marilyn enjoyed herself, joining in the party talk and games.

The point is, when she entered, she did not look like Marilyn Monroe. She was totally, mysteriously, unrecognizable, as if she had stepped into the reality of her true self, Norma Jean Baker. She was fully at ease outside the Hollywood image, but that image was to be her life, and death; ironically, she needed it in her struggle for self-realization.

She liked the neighborhood, and visited here often. On several occasions an old friend, Arthur Miller, who lived nearby was also visiting. It was here, at a party in this high-ceilinged living room, that she lifted an edge of the psychic curtain to reveal some inner demons. I watched her seated on the windowsill, the window open, sipping her drink and staring moodily down to the street below. She was floating off in her daydream, out of contact, gripped by thoughts that could not be pleasant. I went up to her and said softly, "Hey, psst, come back."

She turned. "I'm going to have sleep trouble tonight. I feel it coming. I'm thinking it's a quick way down from here." I nodded because it was a fact. And what could one reply? She continued, "Who'd know the difference if I went?" I answered, "I would, and all the people in this room who care. They'd hear the crash." She laughed, and we made a pact that if either of us was about to jump from a high place, or take the gas or rope or pills, he or she would phone the other and talk the other out of it. We made the pact jokingly; I felt that one day I would get a call, and become a hero. I did get a call, on the last afternoon of her life, but it was masked in a false innocence, and besides I was 3,000 miles away and in no position to prevent the tragedy.

Perhaps at events such as this the rumor arose that I was the man who had introduced Miller to Monroe. Lovers meeting beneath the Brooklyn stars—perfect Manhattan gossip! Though I protested it was not true (they had actually met some time earlier in Hollywood), the story would not go away. Nothing short of an earthquake will shake the rumor, if that. It appears and reappears like an old wives' tale, as mythology, as the kind of fabrication that is needed to establish a Love Story. Intrigue in Brooklyn, followed soon after by Happiness. I've gone down in history as the Man Who ... and nothing will change it. So be it.

Word of her visit to my house spread quickly. Everybody heard about it. The landlord, a quiet man who kept to himself, also heard about it. My stock rose. I was suddenly known as a brilliant writer. Marilyn helped spread this judgment, bless her, whenever she could. The landlord, a cynic toward humanity in general, casually inquired as to her next visit.

"Sometime next week, not sure what day exactly," I said. "And look at the lobby and hallway in the house. Have you been there lately?"

"Are you going to bring up the painting again?" he asked rudely.

"The lobby hasn't been painted in five years. Is that the kind of lobby Marilyn Monroe has to walk through to get to my apartment? It's disgraceful to this house."

He said nothing, but the next day, two painters arrived, spread their drop cloths, and began to work on the lobby. By the following evening he dark corridor was bright with new color. Fluorescent lighting was installed.

I met him several days later. "Do you think she'll like it?" he asked, with his first smile of the year. "I don't want her to think this is a slum house."

The landlord never requested to meet Marilyn. But another Brooklyn man yearned to. He was Benny, who operated a gas station just off Atlantic Avenue. We were friends from the day he lightheartedly sold me gas well under the retail price because I recommended a musical which gave him a glimpse of bosoms and thighs he had not seen since the era of burlesque. He believed you saw enough people on the streets with all their clothes on and thought you should go to the theater to see them with at least half their clothes off. If ever I met a reincarnated oversized leprechaun, Benny was it. He came rolling out to meet his customers with a Mickey Rooney smile and a chirping hello; he filled the tank with good cheer along with gas. The writer's life, whatever that was, intrigued him. "If I had your life . . . " he would say in a dreamy voice, and I'd cut him off with "And if I had yours."

"You'd want mine? Are you crazy? You like the smell of gas?"

"You forget I worked in a gas station as a kid on weekends and summers. I loved it. I fixed flats, greased cars when it was called grease and not lube."

This didn't impress him. "But you got a chance with your life to make it big, Hollywood, women, swimming pools—"

"Ben, listen to me—but first, you're overflowing the tank."

"Gas is cheap, and I give you cut-rate anyway."

"So, I tried Hollywood for a while—"

"And you liked a garage better, heh?" He grinned sardonically.

"That's right."

"You need a head doctor."

"The only head doctor I have is a good dentist."

He raised his arms in despair, spilling additional gas. "How about five dollars?" He added quickly, "I get extra gas free from the dealer, I'm passing it on to you. They give you extra because of evaporation in my underground tanks."

"Then I'm doing you a favor. It would evaporate anyway."

"That's right. Use it or lose it." He grinned at this borrowed show of wit, then lowered his voice. "I see in the papers that Marilyn Monroe is in New York. You know her, right?"

"I know her, right."

He sighed. "What I would give to meet that woman, just once, to say hello and see her smile."

"What would you give?" I asked cruelly.

"A year's free gas."

I followed him into his office, littered with tools, used parts, carburetors, water pumps, assorted small-repair debris. "Jimmy's Garage down the line, y'know what he's got in his office? A Monroe nude calendar. He says he could get a hundred clams for it, but he won't sell. He says his wife comes down to look at it, she's a great fan."

I paid then for my real and evaporated gas in the tank. "I'll bet you want me to try and get a calendar for you. I won't, you're too horny for that. I'll do something else. Maybe have you meet her."

"Where? I'll go anywhere, maybe at your house, if your wife wouldn't object. I'd even go to Manhattan. Anywhere!" His eyes sparkled.

"We'll see. Meanwhile, don't lose any sleep. Be seeing you, Benny." He raised his hand in a sad salute as my Falcon roared away. One thing about Benny, he never made fun of my rust-spotted bird. A true gentleman was Benny.

Marilyn would sometimes drive down to Brooklyn (she was a Bridge person) to visit us and escape from the inner-city pressures. We consider ourselves the outer city. There is no mid city: you're either in or out of Monster Manhattan. She drove down in a white open Cadillac, in her favorite disguise of dark glasses and bandanna. We all had coffee and chocolate cake (her gift to me) and she stayed until our daughter came home from school. After they exchanged the small talk of children, Marilyn made a phone call and announced she was driving back.

"I'll take you to your car," I said. Kisses all around and she and I left.

At her car, I asked, "Have you a few minutes before you take off? Such as a small detour?"

"Whatever you say. You're my brother, did you know that?" She said this with an earnestness that might have destroyed others but left me unharmed; it was that way between us.

"Well, if not a lover, Marilyn, a brother is next best." She giggled. It was a compromise any wise man would settle for.

We were moving down the street. I said, "I want to buy you some gas, just in case."

"Anything for a buddy. Where do I turn?"

Minutes later, a white Cadillac with two passengers, one beautiful, the other dutiful, drove into Ben's Garage and pulled up at a pump. Wiping his hands on a soiled rag, Benny scrambled out of his den. Halfway to the car, he stopped.

"Hey, Benny. We don't need any gas. How about water, oil, and air?" Marilyn and I laughed. Benny remained transfixed, then he approached, a pixie smile dancing about his lips.

"You're Marilyn. Who else? And you came by to see me. I mean, he brought you, I didn't expect you to come on your own. I'm happy to meet you, Marilyn. You're a beautiful person." Benny could say it like that, without pose or artifice, what used to be called straight from the heart. Marilyn was charmed. She reached a hand over the door and offered it to his own dirt-stained hand. He accepted it with sunny grace. "Pleased to meet you, Benny." His name coming from her lips further mesmerized him, but he suddenly shook off that stance and became himself, as she herself.

"Am I dreaming?" he said gaily.

"If you are, so am I. I guess we're both awake."

"Marilyn," he asked, as though this were one moment in a long chatty afternoon, "what's with you and Arthur Miller? With all the stuff in the papers, what can we believe? Are you going to marry him?"

She did one of her little-girl laughs. "I don't know. He hasn't asked me."

"That's not very smart of him."

"He's married, you know, which leaves him out, don't you think?"

"Of course, if he doesn't ask, how can a girl know, eh?" They both laughed softly. I sat quietly in the great Cadillac seat and marveled at the scene. The glamour queen and the garage operator. Marilyn was in that pre-star area she knew so well, the ease and friendliness of ordinary people. Another car drove in for gas, Ben didn't move.

"Hey, there's a customer," Marilyn said.

"Who needs another customer when you're here?" When yet another car drove up, he said goodbye and left her. "Come again whenever you're in the neighborhood. The gas is on me!"

She dropped me off at my street corner. "It's sweet of you to do this," I said.

"He's a sweet man. You can tell. I like the way he shook my hand. I forgot his was not very clean and he wasn't afraid to shake mine. He accepted me, trusting me to accept him as he was. I like that. He's a good friend, I can see that."

In her occasional phone calls and infrequent letters she'd often ask me to give her regards to Benny when next I gas up. And Benny not to be outdone, would often remind me to say hello to Marilyn when we meet. Two improbable birds of passage, from California and

Brooklyn, hitting it off for no apparent reason. It must be that Benny had something of the wayward street smarts that helped Marilyn win her struggle for dignity and success. She may have recognized his soiled hand as her own; she too never feared to offer her hand, though ultimately she died for it.

Larry and Lenny

Let's call this a brief salute to two Brooklyn gentlemen (there are still some around) called Larry and Lenny, whose last names we never quite got, but as Casey Stengel would say, you can look it up. They came into my life and the lives of other residents of Remsen Street for what was to be a few weeks and stayed on for three months. They still come around to keep the house from sagging, and when they do, we greet them happily.

It was a case of The Men Who Came To Dinner, and stayed. One winter, a fire hit the premises, and these men were called in to repair the damages in several of the apartments. Handymen—a combination of carpenter, painter plumber, electrician—are generally jacks of all trades but master of none. L & L, as we soon referred to them, were likable young middle-aged chaps whom we certainly didn't expect to be other than the usual hit-and-run type.

One room in my particular apartment which suffered the most damage is a large bedroom, of 1840 vintage, high ceilings, large windows, parquet floors, fireplace, etc. The firemen, their axes at the ready, came in swinging as they're paid to do. They slashed away at elegant window frames, irreplaceable molding, custom-cut carpentry of the nineteenth century; they had to tear up a third of the floor. It was a depressing sight. The architectural spirit of the room had been destroyed.

Into this room came L & L. They groaned, and inspected the damage. They salvaged every piece of lumber, however small, and began their work. The floor was first. The original parquet border had been partially destroyed and could not be replaced, but they created a neat border of their own. As for the unique frame and moldings around the high windows, they scavenged the lumber yard, matched whatever they could, and combined different moldings to closely approximate the original. You could see they had the soul—dare I use the word?—of artists.

Larry, the quieter and better looking (he says) of the two, told me that they loved old houses, and enjoyed working in them, and felt a responsibility toward them. "These buildings are historical," he said, "built by people a century and a half ago who knew how to turn space into beauty. It's a shame to see how many of them are neglected."

Lenny, with his energy and street wisdom, admired the construction but felt it was overbuilt—overkill, he jokingly called it. "There's too much heaviness, too much material everywhere. Look at these doors and windows, too large, like an overweight or overmuscled person. But they knew how to use wood, the most beautiful material. It keeps its life and color for hundreds of years. Look at that floor, or the doors. And what do most people do? They paint it. They take this beautiful material and kill it by covering it with paint."

His voice became excited, almost angry. "They cover it up. America is the land of the coverup, in wood and in politics. It ought to be a crime to paint over wood. Six months in jail for the first offense!" Lenny could be very impassioned about certain things.

The weeks passed. The fire damage was repaired, but they stayed on to paint and refinish several of my floors—floors that finally reflected the true poetry of the wood. They actually came back several times while working elsewhere in the house to admire those floors. They'd say (I overheard them), "Great. Beautiful job. Super." Then I'd pour some glasses of apple cider and we'd have a brief chat (after hours) about wood, women, life, even books!

Meanwhile, the tenants kept reminding them of work to be done in their apartments; and they'd comply after consulting with the management. The tenants at one point plotted to kidnap L & L and hold them hostage, to be released only after all building violations were taken care of. We decided that was illegal, and besides, we wouldn't want to deprive them of their families.

They have completed their work here, but we think of them as sort of heroes. Lenny once said, "We could live in this building for a year and work on it and make it look a little like the mansion it once was." They had done enough to make our lives brighter. The management may not realize it, but it hit the jackpot in L & L. These are men who give out an honest day's labor. When did you see that lately?

For myself, it wasn't quite goodbye, but *au revoir*. Come warmer weather, they're picking me up for a few rounds of golf. That's right; they believe that all work and no play makes a bad job. When I retire, they've offered to take me on the team. I'm not bad with a hammer and nails, sort of. Look out for L & L and N!

Purely Coincidental

Word got out in the neighborhood (probably leaked by my mailman) that I was writing a book about my small corner of the world. I kept denying it because it wasn't wholly true, but my neighbors only smiled more knowingly at me, some with a conspiratorial wink, as if to confide they could be trusted to go along with my obvious deception. They got curiouser and curiouser. What they wanted to ask—and often did—was the simple question, "Am I in it?" or the other simple question, "Can I be in it?" To which I would reply with the simple answer, "You are not in it," or "I doubt if you can be in it." It didn't stop them. "I have a funny scene if you'll put me in it." Or, "I know of a wife switch in the next block which I can tell you about if you put me in the book."

Ah, scandal. Nothing more likely to cause a writer to lift his drowsy head from his napping board. "If I put you in the book," I would tell an eager one, "I'll have to get a release, a legal form which forbids you ever to sue me."

The mad one laughs gleefully. "Never, I'd never sue you."

"But how do you know what I'll write about you?"

"Anything you say, anything would be fine!" he babbles.

"I couldn't use your real name," I tell him.

Now I've touched his very soul, his aching psyche, the identity *angst*. He begs me, if not on his knees, then in a pronounced stoop, "Please, you must use my real name. I want you to. What's the point if you don't? I want my friends to see my name in a book, even my wife. I can always say the incident is made up. After all, isn't it a novel?" I say I will consider this, and send him on his homeward way chuckling happily.

Then, conversely, or perversely, there is the neighbor who fears the possibility of being mentioned. Although we have been friendly for years, he now says very little, mumbles a lot, offers no information and little gossip, fearing that I will use him in some nefarious way. Often, when he sees me approaching at one end of our street he hurries quickly into his building.

Then there is the work itself, the projected novel, in which the neighborhood is a crucial factor, a sort of Greek chorus. It not only comments, but intrudes. It is not the actual neighborhood, but a mythic counterpart, or to paraphrase Marianne Moore's image, real people in an imaginary garden. To put it another way, the neighborhood—neighbors included—is the scaffolding upon which the author constructs his fiction. Now, people don't like to be called scaffolding, but it's an honorable aid in any construction. When it's over, we carefully dismantle it for possible use later on.

The problem the author is trying to work out in his book is the comic relation between himself and an environment. The neighborhood is the block of clay out of which he tries to mold his figures; but the clay resists, it doesn't particularly want to be molded, it would rather go on as before. Compounding the difficulty is the problem of converting the unresponsive clay into fiction. It is commonplace to say that art is based on life, which is like saying that life originated from the sea—the process is long, complicated, miraculous, and in the end inexplicable. The neighborhood itself is of course unaware of the process wrought upon it by the outside, the writer's eye. It is the struggle to stay, leave or return, that is the classic struggle. If Ulysses didn't want to get home, we'd never have The Odyssey.

When the work is done, this life/art agitation subsides; life is quickly bored by art. Ulysses might have said upon reading Homer, "That really isn't me, that isn't the way it happened at all," and my neighbor might say when the book is out, "I never told you that, you're a liar to say I tormented my wife." To which I would reply, "I never said you tormented your wife, and anyway that isn't you. But if the thought bothers you, it's because you like the idea of tormenting your wife and will probably begin doing it tomorrow."

Nothing will stop this syndrome. Even the cat who sits on the corner of my desk, purring as I write, is confident that it's a book about her. When I look up to think of a line, she meows.

This is Your FBI

I passed Jerry on the street the other day as he leaned against the iron fence fronting the church. "I got some funny news for you, if you can call it that," he said with his usual snicker; it seemed Jerry never got off a real full-throated laugh. He motioned me to one side. He was the local insurance agent, and numbered some biggies among his clients. Though frail-looking, he was a vigorous sports enthusiast and daily jogger; he liked to play handball with the kids on weekends at the outdoor schoolyard.

"So . . . what's the message, Jerry."

"You'll like this, kiddo. First, let me ask did you ever get into trouble with the government? I mean small stuff, drugs, maybe running girls over the Queens border for immoral purposes, heh?" He almost laughed at that one.

"I don't recall any brush with the Feds," I said impatiently. Jerry was not one to get to the point.

"I won't keep the suspense like you literary guys do. After all, this isn't a story but it could be one, given the setting."

"Okay, Jer. I'm late for my barber."

Jerry was a tough neighbor to shake. "Right. So the other day I get a visit from the FBI. Two Harvard-type guys, very polite, they flash the badge like on TV. Can they come in and ask me a few questions? Be my guest, I said. They sit down, one fella takes out a little notebook the other fella leans back, and pops the first question. 'Do you know an Arthur Miller?' to which I reply, 'yes.'"

"Isn't he one of your clients?"

"From way back. But what do they want and what the hell do I really know? Miller moved from the neighborhood long ago. He was some kind of Communist and I guess the FBI—"

"Why do you say he was a Communist?" I was getting annoyed at Jerry's blather. "That was only a rumor."

"I'm only saying what was in the papers back then."

Jerry looked pained. "Sure, maybe you're right. So we talked for a few minutes, how I sold him insurance, property and personal, and how we'd have a cup of coffee once in a while. They asked if he talked about politics. I said I had no recollection, which was the truth."

"Didn't they want to know about you?" I asked.

"Me? I'm clean as a skinned chicken. What's there about me that was subversive? Never belonged to anything except the glee club in high school. Then I got interested in girls and who needed politics? Now here's the stinger. The guy with the little notebook turns to me and says, do I know—and he names you. First I thought he meant the other Norman, he's a client too. But they meant you. Surprise, heh?"

"What did you say?" For once Jerry was right. I was surprised.

"I said, yes, I knew you. You're a buddy. You're a poet and a handball player too. I said we play handball on weekends on the courts down in Red Hook. They looked at me sort of funny. Nobody said nothing. The guy closed his notebook. They both got up, thanked me, and left. What do you make of it?"

"Well, they knew I know Miller, and if he's a communist, then I am too, get it? Guilt by association, which includes you too." And I poked him sharply in the ribs, hoping to crack one.

"All I could think of was the handball. You don't mind that I told them? I couldn't lie."

"No, Jerry. That's fine. Handball is a good old American game. I don't think the Russians know that game at all. And how could a handball player be a spy?"

"So you're clean."

"As a skinned chicken."

"So how about this weekend for a couple of fast singles?"

"If the weather's right, yeah, give me a call. I don't like to play in the rain."

"Hey," Jerry suddenly perked up, "remember when we used to shovel away the snow and play doubles with Barker and Marty Kupperman? With gloves, before the paddles..."

I had taken several steps away before he had finished the sentence, and waved weakly to him. Alone, I thought of the incident and felt unhappy. I had lived through some wild political times, and was very easy with my signature, lending it to causes ranging from Black Action, Open Housing, Vietnam Out, Free the Mexican Wetback, Council for American-Soviet Conciliation, Nuclear Freeze, and a dozen other enterprises sworn to promote brotherhood, alleviate world hunger, end police brutality, denounce Philippine murder, etc. Some of these touched on communist conspiracies, real or imagined, at which point the FBI, real or imagined, would take notes, Xerox newspaper items and files, and generally play the drums of subversion. I didn't mind being on their lists, it proved that I was not totally asleep during my younger years, and action done publicly was public knowledge. Fair enough, though foul it often could be.

I didn't mind any of that. But they had finally found me out. My game of handball was for decades a very personal thing. I did not want to share it with anyone except a few close friends and other players. My skill on the court had a mystical quality to me, a sense of power dissipated if it became known. The whole incident angered me.

I phoned my jolly barrister. "Lawrence, how difficult is it to get a personal item stricken from an FBI report?"

"Forget it. Just pay your rent and don't get arrested for anything."

"Can such an item be removed? Yes or no."

"Yes. It will take years and cost a hundred thousand dollars and mean absolutely nothing. Tell me, did you steal, copy or ever transmit military secrets for or to the Russians?"

"No."

"Did you ever disseminate pornographic material that could be used against your country?"

"They got me down as a handball player. That's invasion of privacy. It's unconstitutional. I want to sue. Will you handle the case?"

"Listen, I gotta rush, Kathy's waiting for me, burning with desire. Take two aspirins and call me tomorrow!"

The Garage Connection

And it came to pass one evening after I had tenderly berthed my car between a Mercedes and a lowly Ford and was crossing Cadman Park that I ran into Melvin, long past garage hours. He was staring into the window of a florist shop; his after-work clothes gave him the look of a small town salesman.

I stopped. "Is that you, Mel?"

He turned, startled. "Hullo. What're you, out for a walk?"

"Just parked my dying Falcon. Who are the flowers for?"

"Nothin'. Just . . . somebody's graduation, friend of my daughter." He seemed embarrassed to be discovered this way. "Listen, you're not still bothered about that replaced radiator hose, are you?"

"No. I think it made the car run better."

He grinned. "You'd make a good salesman, you got the blarney. You might even be good in a garage. Anyway, stop worrying about your old heap. Bet you five it won't pass the next inspection."

"Did I tell you the car was stolen six months ago, but it crawled back just to pass your inspection, would you believe?" He warmed to me a little and we both laughed.

"Old cars keep new cars from being sold," he said. "Truth is, I'm sick of cars, old, new, the whole business." He shifted from one foot to the other. "Which way you walking?"

"At this hour, home. But I'm in no hurry." We started down Henry Street. "I'm walking off some emotional dyspepsia."

"Is that a disease?"

"Just a friendly little argument. Walking can help you figure it out."

He chuckled. "I thought writers lived happily ever after."

"That's only in their books."

We walked along in silence, but I sensed he wanted to speak.

He cleared his throat. "May as well tell you, I didn't stop at that florist to buy flowers, except maybe for my wife, then it seemed too corny. She wouldn't believe it." He took a long breath. "I have problems at home. Nothing serious, she ain't walking out, but something's wrong. It might be a small thing like someone's jealous, or being selfish which we all are, y'know?"

"I'm sorry to hear it. She's a nice woman, I only meet her now and then. . . ."

"She thinks you're okay, being a writer and all that. She even got one of your books out of the library. So anyway . . ." He came to a halt, and turned to me. "Now that I ran into you, maybe you can help. Let me put it this way, like if I could tell her how I feel about her, that I think she's a fine person, it might help. But I couldn't tell her. But suppose you write something, could you do that? Since her birthday's comin' up—"

"You mean write something *for* you?"

"No, you write it for her, and I give it to her, with her birthday and all. For example, if you could write her a short poem—"

"I don't know about that—"

"You're a writer, aren't you?" He kicked at the patch of grass like a big kid. "It's got to have the feeling I really feel for her if I could write, except it's your little gift. I'll say I happened to mention your birthday, and you volunteered, instead of a birthday card. What do you think?" He regarded me warily.

"It's a nice idea, but I'm not sure I can do it."

"Isn't that what poets do, write poetry?"

"Not to order. But then again, why not?"

His face lighted with anticipation. "It might change things, sort of break the ice. I know you could do a nice job, like it wasn't you flirting with her, but speaking for a buddy." He saw me waver, and added, "I'll go easy on the next inspection, except for the brakes."

"Let's not worry about brakes. Okay, I'll have a try. I'll write something short, like a sonnet."

He was eager now, and happy. "Is that poetry, a sonnet?"

"The best, if you do it right. Shakespeare wrote over a hundred. Well, I'm jogging the rest of the way. See you at the end of the week."

"And bring—what'd you call it, a sonnet!"

My dyspepsia was fading. I doubled back to the florist where I bought half a dozen roses. Ten minutes later my wife was startled to see me coming through the door with flowers.

"What's this all about? My birthday is months past."

"Would you like roses, or a sonnet still to be written?"

"Right now, the roses. Aren't they lovely!"

"Good choice. Because the sonnet is promised to another woman."

"That's exciting, dear. Anyone I know?" she asked, sorting the flowers as she gave me a mischievous look.

"I don't think so. It's more or less a commissioned piece. The husband thinks it might help their marriage. Too complicated to explain."

"These are lovely, guilt offering or no. You're sweet to bring them." She reached for a vase. "I hope you write a beautiful sonnet. Bring the lovers into each other's arms."

Which is what I did, from what I hear. Fine with me. I can't write about the Brooklyn Bridge all the time.

Night of the Dog

While animals in any neighborhood are aplenty, the case of the hundred-year-old dog (fourteen years on the human scale) could not go unnoticed in this part of the Brooklyn forest. A lady dog, who had lost her male companion of ninety-four, may be no unusual event in the dog world, but we humans, often bored with human interest, look to other species.

Her name is Hunca Munca (see Beatrix Potter) and all of her fourteen—oops, hundred—years have been with the same owner and in the same apartment. Ann (owner) had loved and been loved in return by her two terriers, and a year after the surviving Hunca went over the fourteen-year barrier, it was determined that on a certain day quite soon she would—on our time span—have reached the century mark. And she did.

Time for a birthday party!

Now a birthday party for a dog is no small matter, even for a small dog. In this case, the dog had innumerable admirers; there was no room to invite them all. It was decided to parade Hunca in the lobby beforehand to greet her well-wishers.

"She will have a special bath," Ann insisted.

"And I will have to hold her in the tub."

"Yes, thank you. That would be helpful. She knows you and will be less of a problem." Ann is very efficient and has a smile that would draw a bee away from honey.

I volunteered to be on the organizing committee, but did not know how one organizes a birthday party for a canine. A canine, one might add, who is quite deaf and half blind, as befits a centenarian. As the day of the celebration approached, Hunca wouldn't be a dog if she didn't sniff out a plot. Her bubble bath was a tipoff; then the unusual housecleaning; she sensed that something new was going to happen.

The day arrived. First, there was a longer than usual dog-walk. She was allowed an unlimited sniffing time among shrubs, a heavenly indulgence. Then, back upstairs, the morning biscuit mysteriously became two. A haircut followed, administered with a sweet song. Something's up, Hunca thought, and took a short nap. Upon waking, her hair was tenderly brushed, then a pretty ribbon tied around her neck. The fuss must be about me, whatever it is, she must (or could) have thought. She ran about the room as visitors arrived, wagging her tail and bumping into people and the furniture. Little gifts were deposited on the rug: biscuits, small milk bones, doggie toys and, baked especially for this occasion by a neighbor next door, a large chocolate cake. Hunca set on Ann's lap while another neighbor with a camera took a dozen snappy Polaroids of Hunca who, to tell the truth, was getting a bit sleepy. Candles were placed on the cake. She stared at them dreamily, and took a sly lick at the frosting. Then it was time to read my poem in her honor.

I called her name sharply. She snapped her ears to alert, looked directly at me (I had often given her a biscuit) while in my best oratorical manner I delivered my tribute, the first ever, to a dog.

> We are gathered here tonight
> to celebrate, you wouldn't believe it—
> words fail me—I give you
>
> Hunca Munca, creature extraordinaire,
> so blithe, cuddly, and fair;
> in short, a dog. Sound the clarion,
> she's a real live centenarian!
>
> Last year it was the Brooklyn Bridge;
> this year, Hunca Munca.
> Can you hear me, ole Hunc?
> You're one hundred on our human calendar,

or if it's any comfort to you,
we would be fourteen on yours.

How to celebrate you, darlin' lady?
Though you're half blind,
and more than a bit deaf, you're still ready
to chase a biscuit down the hall.
After a bath you're radiant,
your coat mysteriously soft and white.

You're propped on a pillow
like a stuffed baby polar bear (small size),
paws up and folded, nose black, eyes
staring into space and maybe smiling.
Lovable enough to kiss (ugh),
dreaming of peeing unmolested
on the green meadow of carpet.
Dream on, Hunca, at age 100,
live to your heart's desire,
you can't go much higher.

In the next world (are you ready?)
you'll be adored, chucked under the chin,
surrounded by heavenly cherubim
who'll wonder who you are
until someone says,
That's Hunca Munca, the hundred-year movie queen,
and ain't we lucky to get her?

Stay clean, Hunc.
Stay off junk.
Stick with your biscuit.
And Happy Birthday as you doze
in your pretty white clothes.

It was also the first time I ever put a dog to sleep with my poetry,
though I had often accomplished this feat before with people.

City Cop

The trouble started when Rick found out he was going to be a first-time father. Up till then he was the usual street cop and not your usual dumb type; more on the soft-spoken, warm-hearted side, a man quick on the smile and I'll bet slow on the draw (I doubt he ever pulled a gun on anyone).

This may be talking out of school, but he could be retired by now and what harm in showing a man could be human while wearing the shield? He'd push my buzzer in the early AM, stick his head in the hallway and call up, "I'm sweeping your block in ten minutes. Move your Sherman tank!" He meant my car, bless him. Rick believed in the law, but he hated to give out parking tickets, especially to friends, and he had lots of friends in the neighborhood. He understood their frustration, the absurdity of penalizing the motorist while not providing enough places to park. He knew that parking tickets had to be given out, but it pained him to do it. He tried dodges, such as ticketing the streets ten to twenty minutes after the zero hour on the signs, allowing the sleepyheads extra time to roll out of their beds and get their cars to safety.

He would be capable of leaving a note tucked under the wiper, such as, "I enjoyed your article in Holiday Magazine." Except the note would be about the size of a parking ticket and from a distance as I walked toward my car I thought I had got one, cursing Rick and later feeling guilty about it.

He'd watch the scramble of cars for spaces each morning. "If this is civilization, let's climb the trees and join the monkeys," he'd say as we crossed briefly at the corner, I wondering about the police getting fat on bribes and he about the money writers were supposed to be making. Then, slapping his summons book, he turned to his sordid business, a man condemned to inflict pain upon his fellow citizens. I never asked him to fix a ticket; except when I got one for a hydrant violation, I went to him for advice. "I'm going to court on this. I was nowhere near that hydrant, and I'm sore about it. I'm going to tell the truth!"

"Whoa, hold it," he said. "No one knows what the truth is, especially in court, and you can't prove it anyway. That you were over ten feet from the hydrant? How much over? Did you have a tape measure and measure the distance? Did you have a camera with you and by luck was able to take a shot? No. And there goes the truth."

"But I only ran into the store for a newspaper—"

"So you ran into the store to get laid, to visit your sick grandmother, to catch a quick fix, to look at the new crotch mags—the judge don't care. He's heard it all before, he's heard five thousand stories. If he could write he'd write a book, he hopes."

"But the truth is—"

"What you need is a new story, not too corny." He paused. "I got it. You're a skier, right?"

"Right."

"So you're writing all week and you get away to ski. Now you get back, your skis on top of your car, and you park near but not in front of the hydrant, to drop your skis off at your house. You have a friend in that building, basement floor, while you live next door in a three-flight walkup, so you keep your skis where it's easier to get. Okay. You park for a minute or two to get the skis off the rack and into the house. Two, three minutes the most, you have to lock the skis in the basement what with all the crime. You come out, there's the ticket." He stopped. "You don't like it?"

"I don't know."

"First place, they don't often have a ski story in court, and it's kind of fancy. I mean, how many genuine skiers appear in court anyway? They send in the fine. You're not rich, so you throw yourself on the mercy of the court."

"It sounds like I'm up for execution."

"The point is, it could be the truth, if you believed it. The judge might buy it."

The judge bought it.

Now when Rick found out he was going to become a father, there was no more idle gossip about traffic tickets and baseball. And I was no longer going to *him* for advice; he was coming to *me*. Because I was already a father; maybe he figured if I survived, so would he. The future worried him; the mysterious creature soon to be born filled his days with anxiety. "What's it like?" he would ask.

"What's what like?"

"Having a kid around all the time."

"It's sleeping most of the time the first couple of years, you won't have to worry."

"But it cries a lot, they tell me."

"You wear ear stoppers."

"And all those diapers." He smiled weakly.

"We all started with diapers, Rick. Even you. Just let nature run its course. Relax."

"Why can't I be like Elaine? She's enjoying it."

Elaine was delighted with her pregnancy, she was hopeful, happy, and looking forward to the event even as Rick grew more fearful. I'd say to Elaine when we'd meet in the deli line, "What's with the man these days?" and she'd laugh merrily. "He's worried I might have twins, sort of double trouble. The situation will change when the baby comes."

It did and it didn't. That is, Rick was slightly awed by the event when it arrived, and expressed his wonderment. "Did you ever notice a baby's fingers? I mean the fingernails?"

"You mean they're very small," I answered.

"The hands and fingers are *small*. The fingernails are *tiny*, like a . . . a tiny seashell." He seemed pleased by the image.

"So things are working out?"

"Sort of, but the nights are awful. I don't get the sleep I need. And I promised to take one of the feedings." His voice dropped. "Elaine talked me into it."

"It could be fun, once in a while."

"Sure, once in a while, but every night, Jesus . . . I'm losing weight."

"Well, Ricky, after six months it'll ease up."

He groaned. "You mean it'll go on for six months?"

I gripped his arm. "It'll go on forever."

I shouldn't have said it, I suppose. The idea of permanent fatherhood seemed to throw him. He'd often be morose, even sullen, when I'd drop by to see the baby. In six months the boy was crawling all over the place. Rick admitted he enjoyed playing with Tommy, but the kid was too noisy, and toys were getting underfoot. The place became a nest of booby traps, he complained. Through it all, Elaine kept her sunny spirit. Somehow this bothered Rick; he wanted her to suffer along with him; she wouldn't. Tommy went from crawling to walking, Elaine was radiant whenever we met; Rick was approaching depression.

"I can't seem to snap out of it," he said to me over an off-duty pizza in a local deli. "Could it be someone that size can upset my life this much? For instance, Elaine is a honey and I love her, but she's too tired to love *me*, y'know? That kid is interfering with my sex life. What am I gonna do?"

"Nothing."

"You think so, heh?" he growled. "You're wrong. I can pack them both off to her mother and wait it out until he leaves for college."

"Come on, Rick."

"I can't take it," he said morosely. "The thing is, couple of months ago I thought of quitting the force, get into some other work, maybe more money. Now with the kid here, I'll have to stick where I am, job, pension, the old family trap." He offered a weak smile. "Maybe I wasn't cut out for being a parent."

"Nobody is cut out for that," I said and meant it. "It's an unnatural state. Look at the animals, they're not parents."

"You're right." He ate in silence for a moment. "Elaine says if we hang on he'll be in nursery school before we know it."

"Yeah, except that's not out into the world, it's a few block away, then he's home again. I told you it's hopeless."

"I thought it was me who told you it was hopeless," he said hopelessly. We brooded about this for a moment. "I wouldn't have imagined it, just having a baby. After all, Elaine had it, I was a dumb innocent bystander. The question is, will things ever get back to normal again?"

"When he goes away to camp, maybe." I just couldn't seem to say the right things to help a troubled friend.

He looked at his watch. "I better get home. Elaine likes me around to help with the kid."

"And you never could resist a woman in need of help."

"That's a fact. That's how I met Elaine. She was fixing a flat at the side of the road, and I slowed down and stopped." He smiled a bit, then remembered the issue at hand. "Then the kid had to come along."

"Just remember he might grow up and love you for stopping."

Rick's eyes widened, the idea overwhelming him.

The week following, at a late hour, he dropped by the house, looking haggard and disorganized. "Could you put me up for the night? She didn't exactly throw me out, just threw a plate." He sat on the couch, visibly upset. "Where's the wife?"

"She sacked out early. No problem, Rick. The couch is yours, and breakfast."

"I'll slip out early, thanks. It's got me down, that's all. Seems like she and the kid are both turning against me. Or am I goin' crazy?"

"Does she know you're here? I'll phone her and find an excuse. You look awful. Why don't you wash up and I'll get the blankets, okay?"

In the movies you'd have calendar leaves falling, each a year, but here I will merely say that six or seven years passed, and the Tommy tide began to turn. One day, Rick brought over a folder of drawings to show me. Animals, landscapes, an ocean with whales, and one frightening pen-and-ink sketch of a face with the mouth opening to shout a command or swallow a small bird whole. He held up the sketch.

"That's me when I yell at him."

"At Tommy?"

"He says that's how I look when I yell. He calls me the monster." Rick laughed heartily. "Me! He calls me that to my face. The monster! How about that drawing, eh? What a kid."

All I could do was shake my head and marvel. Rick now behaving like a proud daddy!

Again, as we'd cross in our neighboring duties, he working toward a pension, I toward immortality (would it were reversed), I would hear a continual stream of praise for Tommy. "He got two hits in the school baseball game. Including a home run. How about that, hey?"

"Talented, for sure."

"You ought to see his marks. Not just a dumb athletic type. His teacher gives him an A on all his compositions. He's college material, wouldn't you say? There's a story for you!" Rick had reached the euphoria of expectation. Every six months he'd bring up the subject—a story about Tommy. I said he wasn't a story yet, just a subject. But Rick kept pressing me.

I'd say, "He hasn't done anything great yet. He's just a kid. There's no story yet."

"Make one up."

"Don't you want a true story?"

"Well, make it a true story. Come on, he deserves it."

"I'll think about it."

"The kid's a genius."

"And you're a monster."

He exploded into laughter. He leaned against a tree and laughed wildly. "Imagine," he sputtered, "he had the guts to call me that. To my face! You got to love a kid like that."

Well, you could try. I guess Rick did.

Flash: Michael Palin
Crosses the Brooklyn Bridge

I was surprised, upon meeting the renowned world traveler Michael Palin in Manhattan, to discover he had never visited Brooklyn, that fabled land south and slightly to the east. As the Monty Python seer explained it, "I know it's there, shrouded in myth, but I never got up the courage to visit. Or I was never invited. It is a real place, Brooklyn, you say?"

I assured him it was indeed, and invited him to visit. I thought it part of my official duties to encourage famous people to look in on us. Boss Howard Golden would be pleased, and I continue drawing my dollar-a-year stipend.

"How does one arrive in Brooklyn?" Michael asked eagerly, like a boy who had cut school for the day. "There's the tube, I assume. One doesn't fly in, does one?"

I said, "For those who consider Brooklyn part of Long Island, which it is, and where the American General George Washington retreated from your King's troops two hundred years ago, you can now fly in via Kennedy Airport. Otherwise, there's the automobile, the tube, or subway as we call it, possibly small boat or canoe, and yet another way known to the relatively few, especially foreigners."

"Do go on."

"You can walk to Brooklyn."

"Over water?" he asked jovially.

"Over the Bridge."

"How jolly. Let's bloody do it!"

Michael didn't quite talk that way, but having impressed one another with our wit, we got down to simple declarative sentences.

"Okay, Michael, why not the Bridge today?"

Michael reflected the gung-ho spirit that once built an empire. He was wearing Nike sneakers (his traveling shoes, he explained) and in neat jeans and snappy sweater proved to be an expert walker. Walking a famous bridge is not the same as walking a famous avenue. As the bridge's parabola rises, and you rise with it, walking the curve, something in the spirit rises, the water below glistens, you walk into the net of girders and cables, into a mysterious web of time. The Bridge does it to those with risible spirits.

The madcap Monty Python spirit, as reflected in the body of Michael Palin, could soar indeed. Michael was overcome with awe, as I expected him to be; it was, and still is for me, an awesome experience. He kept mumbling (with a British accent) "Marvelous, marvelous," and kept turning his head for a backward look after each hundred paces, to get the changing perspectives. It proved to me he was a natural bridge fancier. He knew the world was round (not quite realized by most people) and the earth's movement subtly affected everything upon it, whether stable or in motion.

At the center span, we rested and looked out over the water, sky above, clouds drifting, the city's power throbbing on the horizon but leaving this arc of serenity undisturbed. I closed my eyes. Some lines of Whitman fluttered through my head. "Cross from shore to shore, countless crowds of passengers!/Stand up, tall masts of Mannahatta! Stand up, beautiful hills of Brooklyn! . . . /We receive you with free sense at last, and are insatiate henceforward . . . ." Then I thought of this Bridge, this fabulous gift of an earlier century, a decade in the making; nothing to compare with it has been built in America. I knew that the towers of the suspension bridges built in the twentieth century are of steel, and that the towers of the Brooklyn Bridge are both the first and the last of the monumental stone gateways on the North American continent. I thought of Washington Roebling who took over the design and labor of his father and watched his creation grow from year to year, rising ghostlike, under the severest engineering difficulties, across the East River; then himself stricken through the last years of construction, confined to bed and chair, watching the progress from the window of his Heights apartment, observing through binoculars the day-by-day raising of the miracle. For it would be called an engineering miracle, acknowledged the world over. And when Roebling was unable to carry on, his wife Emily took over the task, as able and valiant as any man. She implemented her husband's directives, and guided the final, exhausting labors to the day of triumph. Engineers would later say, at its centennial, that with normal maintenance and certain minimal replacement of parts, "it will last forever."

I thought of myself and the Bridge, sharing my daily life with it: to be near it, on it or under it; bicycle over it; walk over it; rest or sleep on the curved wooden benches; see it in the spring with sunlight glistening along its curve, or in winter with the cold icing the cables; to observe it in rain, fog, storm, sunrise, dusk, midnight; to see it almost empty or burdened with an endless string of moving cars.

Michael's voice broke my reverie. "Marvelous, unbelievable, tremendous, this bridge."

"You're hooked," I said. "One of the millions lucky or wise enough to take the walk."

"It looks so solid, the cables, the supporting bars and suspenders, and those high stone towers, as solid as anything man could build, yet it seems, as we stand here, weightless, as though it would float away if it weren't moored to the land."

I listened to my British friend with admiration. Yes, he was hooked, he was a bridge freak. "It's like looking over the rim of your Grand Canyon, I suppose," he added, "judging from pictures I've seen. The same unearthly quality."

"Did you know," I said, "in May 1883, the first day it opened, 150,000 people crossed on foot and 1800 vehicles carrying thousands more. People were bridge crazy."

"Someone in a bar once wanted to sell me the Brooklyn Bridge."

"Did you buy it?"

"Yes, but I never did get a receipt."

"You can always buy it again, Michael, it's that kind of Bridge. Did you know there are four main cables, each 3500 feet in length. And what do you suppose is the number of miles of wrapping wire on each cable?"

"Haven't a clue, but go on."

"Two hundred forty-three. And what do you suppose is the length of wire in each cable? It's 3500 miles, the distance from New York to California. But let's forget statistics. Just look at it; strange to look at it when you're on it, maybe that's part of the mystique and wonder. Egypt has its pyramids for the world to look at, but our Bridge has a special American quality: it's not just for show but for use. People walk over it and ride over it, some even picnic on it. History plus utility. Shall we carry on?"

"Good idea, I'm getting hungry," said Michael.

"It's downhill the rest of the way."

I pointed out the other Bridge (Manhattan), the other borough (Queens), the residence of the other Norman (Brooklyn Heights) plus the other tallest building (World Trade Towers). I also pointed out as any good tourist guide such items as Empire State Building and the Statue of Liberty; we caught a glimpse of the Staten Island ferryboats; we slowly descended toward the street ramp with a final view of both boroughs linked by the Bridge.

Brooklyn. Home port. We walked down to the water's edge (Fulton Ferry Landing), snaking back directly under the Bridge—the final astounding image rearing, vaulting over us, the "choiring strings" of its thin and finely spun cables catching the late sunlight, making it gossamer, ghostly. Only the insistent hum of the endless traffic over the span brought it back to our time, back to its physical reality. By then, my companion was numb with surprise and delight. Numb briefly, for he literally did a short dance under that span—would I had a photo to prove it—and announced himself ready for more.

Michael later sent me a postcard with a photo of London Bridge, and the cryptic message, "We've got one too." I forgave his arrogance, and embrace his spirit like a brother.

"Dem Bums"

One bright afternoon, having been defeated at my desk by a poem, I put the monster aside and fled to the handball courts. There, I defeated a charming but tough woman player in a singles game. On my way home, a short jog, I stopped to greet my neighbor the Rev. Donald McKinney, minister of the local Unitarian Church.

Rev. McKinney keeps a low profile in the community, being the kind of man who believes that good deeds and sermons suffice. He is a strong speaker who doesn't seem to be preaching as much as delivering thoughts and impressions to friends. He can be serious or playful, and entertaining if the subject lends to it. Knowing I am a Sunday "irregular" he nevertheless treats me with the respect a passing agnostic deserves. And I treat him with the candor and openness I would a poet or handball player.

He says to me, "I'm giving a sermon this Sunday you wouldn't want to miss, being a lover of sports."

"What's the subject?"

He smiled. "It shall be revealed."

It was indeed, and good enough to be shared. He strode to the pulpit and began:

"I cannot claim to have been a Brooklyn Dodgers fan. From early childhood I was a conditioned Red Sox supporter. Having grown up in the environs of Boston, it could have happened that I became a fan of the Braves, then still in Boston, but it didn't happen that way. And I never had any interest in major league baseball until I came to Brooklyn.

Indeed, the only other passion in me for any other baseball team was total hatred of those damn Yankees, a feeling from which I have never really freed myself. When I came to this church in September of 1952, the only feeling I had about the Dodgers was one of smug disdain. Them bums were really only something to joke about.

"It did not take me long, however, to realize that the Dodgers were no joking matter to the life of Brooklyn. And indeed were to add significant dimension to my ministry here. Although I did not see the Dodgers play until the following June, I could not help being caught up that fall in the fever of one of those incredible subway series between the Yankees and the Dodgers. The Dodgers fully expected to win the series. It went to seven games. But once again, they lost it, as they had so often before.

"Following that crucial seventh game in the 1952 series, in the church office, Gladys Hudson, the wonderful parish assistant, suggested I check up on Miss Ethel Stevens, although it had only been a few days since I had seen her. I, of course, had come to know who Miss Ethel Stevens was and to distinguish her from her sister, Elaine. Both were pillars of the church, both were retired schoolteachers with, however, decidedly different temperaments. When I asked Gladys why I should be in touch with Ethel Stevens, Gladys smiled, shrugged her shoulders, and said, "I just think you should go see her. She must be feeling pretty low." In as much as people usually did what Gladys Hudson told them to do, and especially young new assistant ministers, I got on the BMT that afternoon and went out to Flatbush.

"I found Miss Stevens in bed, looking absolutely awful, and to my untrained eye, possibly dying. There was nothing wrong with her physically. She was simply in total despair. The Dodgers had lost. I had not seen anyone respond to an event of any kind in that way before in my life. I had no idea what to say or do. Fortunately, although at the time I could not begin to imagine how or why a baseball team should have that effect on a very sensible and usually quite jolly lady, I had the wit not to try to make light of this disaster. It was through Ethel Stevens, whom I came to know very well and love dearly that I gradually came to understand and appreciate something of the meaning of the Dodgers in the life of Brooklyn.

"It was she who took me to my first game, on my birthday, an experience I will never forget. Although I now have no idea who the Dodgers were playing that day, and I don't even remember who won, I knew, and not just because of all the cans that were flying all over the place, that I was experiencing something I had never known in Fenway Park, even in the near hysteria that sometimes surrounded Ted Williams. The very atmosphere of Ebbets Field was charged. With what I know not. It wasn't just partisan enthusiasm, although there certainly was plenty of that, or love of baseball; it was something far grander. More special. In that place, for that time, the crowd was empowered by something wonderful and strong. You were made proud of being in Brooklyn, being a great presence, regardless of who and what you individually were outside the walls of Ebbets Field. Ebbets Field, Flatbush, was without doubt the heart, perhaps the soul, of Brooklyn. And it beat with a mighty force. I know that Fenway Park in Boston never had any such role for Bostonians. And I doubt if many ball parks and teams have had such a profound place in the life of a people as did Dem Bums here in Brooklyn.

"It took quite a while before I recognized the full extent of Ethel Stevens's need of, love of, and identification with the Dodgers. Others of you may have responded differently, but she was the one for me to whom the Dodgers became reality. Surely she wasn't embarrassed by her feelings, but I guess she just didn't want to expose them till she was sure enough of me. But gradually and finally I did discover that not only did she learn every single statistic of the Dodgers and every play in every game but she knew and remembered the birthday of every member of the Dodger team. And the wedding anniversaries of all who were married, and furthermore, the birthdays of all their children. When she learned that the teenaged son of one of the less famous, less-well-paid Dodgers had a serious drug problem—and how she found out about it, I never did discover—she came to me and asked if I would direct what in those days was a sizable amount of money through my discretionary fund for the payment of treatment for that boy, whom she in other ways had arranged to get into a clinic in Lexington, Kentucky. Again, she did not want the family to know who had done this or to feel beholden to her as an individual. I don't think she ever had met a single member of the Dodger team. She was always just a fan.

"I started out by saying that I had never been a Dodger fan, and that is true. And perhaps I didn't feel I had the right to. I didn't really belong in Brooklyn in those days—of course, a very, very different Brooklyn from the one we know today. I followed the baseball teams very closely in those remaining five years of the Dodgers' life in Brooklyn, knowing I would have to make periodic sick calls on Ethel Stevens, among other reasons. And, also, coming to realize that the tone and temper of life in this borough, even among those determinedly uninterested in baseball, was affected by how the Bums were doing.

"It was also an understanding of the power of the Dodgers over the heart and mind of Brooklyn that I realized what it meant for the Dodgers to be the team that finally integrated baseball. You may or may not know the full story of that struggle, and it really was a historic, heroic action for Branch Rickey, the inimitable Dodgers' owner, to sign Jackie Robinson. Professional baseball had not started out, as you may know, as a segregated sport. In the early 1880's more than twenty blacks held positions on various leagues throughout the country. However, in 1888, to appease Southern teams, a rule banning "colored" players from organized baseball was passed, and major league baseball remained determinedly lily white until the 1946 season. For Branch Rickey, it was a matter of very deep ethical concern that blacks were not allowed to play in the majors. And he waited and plotted for years for the right moment to move and the right player, who he sensed could and would endure the inevitable hatred and abuse that would be piled on him. Today it is almost impossible to imagine what Jackie Robinson went through only thirty some years ago. And it's hard to imagine today what that meant to Brooklyn, which was then overwhelmingly white, with many strong ethnic neighborhoods, brought together as Brooklyn and Brooklynites only by the Dodgers.

"I am sure it was not so much the innate goodness and moral superiority of Brooklynites that made them quickly rally behind Jackie Robinson, but rather their intense loyalty to the Dodgers; it forced them to stand up for the team against the attacks of the rest of the world, of which there were many. Robinson was followed of course by Roy Campanella, and Don Newcombe, and in the decade from the late forties to 1957, the Dodgers were quite glorious, playing increasingly better baseball, climaxed in 1955 when at long last they finally won the World Series and did it against those Yankees from across the river. I can't imagine anyone living in Brooklyn then who does not remember that day. Fortunately, I was here at the church in the Heights then, could rush out to Borough Hall when that last Yankee was called out and be there at the Dodgers building and personally experience some of that incredible joy, gladness and ecstasy that was this city's on that day. It wasn't pandemonium. There was no chaos, there was just a sense of life being absolutely grand and wanting to share this sense of wonder and fulfillment with everybody who was in Brooklyn.

"There has been no moment like that since. Indeed, in two short years the Brooklyn Dodgers were no more. It was all over. And in very real ways, Brooklyn died. Just as it had known its greatest hour. Even now, almost thirty years later, it is a bit hard to grasp what happened. How could they leave the most supportive fans in all of baseball, accounting in the very year they were sold to Los Angeles for forty percent of all ticket sales in the entire National League?

"The move was the act of the owner, Walter O'Malley, undoubtedly the most deservedly hated man in Brooklyn's history. He wanted to get out of Brooklyn. He lied about receipts. He refused any and all offers to negotiate a new and larger playing field, and employed in the most classically villainous way every possible devious maneuver to get out. Why? Why did he want so desperately to leave?

"Largely, of course, it was pure, unadulterated greed. He got an awful lot of money out of Los Angeles. But he also had a not-at-all-carefully-veiled hatred of blacks. He could not stand what was happening to Brooklyn. In that respect, of course, he was not unlike so many Brooklyn Dodgers fans. It is more than a bit ironic that the same Brooklynites who so stoutly defended Branch Rickey's brave and righteous decision to sign on Jackie Robinson fled in enormous numbers from all the neighborhoods in Brooklyn that were beginning to have black residents. As these old Brooklynites moved by the hundreds of thousands to Long Island and other suburbs, their places were taken by more and more blacks, at first many from the Islands and then many more from the South, who had a very different life-style, and of course as others who had come to Brooklyn before them came, largely in poverty.

"This massive population switch, that started in earnest in the middle 1950's, with the terrible urban blight that inevitably accompanies any such sudden, massive change, cannot be blamed, per se, on O'Malley's taking the Dodgers away. Symbolically, however, the selling of the Dodgers was a deliberate death blow to Brooklyn.

"I announced in the Brooklyn Unitarian that this morning's sermon was to be a theological analysis of the place the Dodgers held in the life and death of Brooklyn. Maybe you don't think that is what I have been doing. To me, the place of the Dodgers in Brooklyn is, however, somewhat and strangely analagous to the old Christian passion story.

"Brooklyn, for generations the poor relation of Manhattan, with so little to think of as its own, the city's principal dumping ground of the poor, needed something like the Dodgers to give form and substance, to give indentity to its people, to provide hope and common life. All those jokes about Brooklyn and Dem Bums that were common in my youth, I realize now were not put-downs, but a special kind of celebration of a people, a people feeling good about themselves needing desperately to find something to feel good about themselves. They needed, and they had a saviour.

"The Dodgers were the substance of a necessary faith, a faith in one's place, one's home, one's surroundings, even if it be with two or more million unknown people who had nothing else in common. The faith that brought them together—the love of Dem Bums.

"I know, however, that one must not make too much of this kind of analogy. After all, there were plenty of loyal, concerned Brooklynites who had no interest in the Dodgers whatsoever. My predecessor for instance, John Lathrop, during his forty-seven years here, attended, I believe, only one Dodgers game, again, at the invitation, or I think in this instance, at the insistence of Miss Ethel Stevens. He had no feelings about the Dodgers at all, not even caring, if I remember correctly, when the Dodgers had won that World Series. It is of course purely coincidental, but it is interesting to note that he did leave Brooklyn for the West at exactly the same time the Dodgers did.

"It was wonderful that Brooklyn had the Dodgers. It was terrible that they were taken from us. Walter O'Malley was a Judas Iscariot, appropriately identified as he was by columnists at the time as belonging in the company of Adolph Hitler and Joseph Stalin.

"No one knows, of course, what Brooklyn might have been like if the Dodgers had stayed. Each year now there are fewer and fewer folk who know even where Ebbets Field stood, what that holy ground meant to people.

"Something terribly precious, a spiritual blessing that was Brooklyn died when the Dodgers left. The soul of Brooklyn was taken. Miss Ethel Stevens, seventy-two years of age when the Dodgers left, lived on another five years. She never seemed quite the same. She never wanted to talk about the Dodgers leaving. The old Brooklyn is dead. So be it. It is still hard to know if there will be a new Brooklyn. I don't think there is such a thing today. There are new stirrings of pride and concern in some neighborhoods. That's good. But there is a great abyss, all those terrible miles of burned out, abandoned buildings, and there is no sense of our being one, even for a passing moment.

"Will something like the Dodgers rise from the ashes? Who knows? Such an essentially spiritual phenomenon can't be plotted or planned or produced by any computerized magic. I think people find symbols and lift them up to help them believe when they have to, when they find, once again, they must believe in the worth of themselves in ways beyond their concern for themselves as individuals. When they need to believe in something more, they will find something to help them with that faith.

"When and how that knowledge or those new symbols come is, I believe, one of those constant mysteries of faith. But I suspect that something in the order of Dem Bums may yet be with us, when we're ready."

Identity Crisis

Friend and press agent Bill phoned unannounced and unsolicited to ask what I was up to, and if I was, what was it, and would it be of literary interest to announce such information?

"I am brooding," I replied, "over the fact that a poet in Maine, convicted of killing his wife, is doing nicely in prison running a poetry workshop. He's gotten two books of poetry published since his imprisonment, while I, who have never even dreamed of killing my wife, or even injuring her, find it difficult to get a new book of poetry published."

"Let's stick to business. Are you working on something new?" Bill asked briskly.

"Actually, rewriting something old."

"The public wants what's new. Is there a new bee in your bonnet?" If nothing else, Bill liked to turn a phrase.

"Aside from rewriting an old, I am yes at work on a new."

"Good!" he exclaimed. "Now we have something to go on. Remember, you have published nothing exciting since your Marilyn Monroe book while the other Norman is racing through his triple trilogy. Does that bother you?"

"No. Should it?"

"Yes. Now, your new work, is it a novel or a play?"

"A long poem."

A long pause. "Your trouble is, you have a death wish. Okay, I can say there's a book in the works, correct?"

"As a matter of fact, Bill, there is. It takes place at the South Pole—for secrecy and media blackout. We have an assemblage of top psychiatrists from every nation on earth, a supranational body meeting in urgent session, worried about the onrushing mass insanity of mankind, and how to cope with it."

"May I refer to it as a love story?"

"It is, in the deepest sense. A husband-wife psychiatric team splits up, she goes for a black Third World stud, which drives white First World husband mad. Madness as the innate human condition, you see? I also include murder, rape, and a Japanese disembowelment. This is my grand push for commerical success."

"I like the general idea. Give me a title, and I'll pass it on to a columnist who needs copy."

"I have no title except, possibly, Myron."

"Give me a firm title by tomorrow. We must restore your Identity, which goes with a title, or a headline event, or an attack by a Women's Organization. One other thing, friend. Have you a business card?"

I bridled at the question, and bared my teeth.

Bill seemed to sense my anger. "I mean a simple physical identity expressed these days by the commonplace query: 'Have you a business card, sir?' Well, have you?"

I had indeed run into that query often in my freelance travels up and down lonely high-speed elevators and through Muzak-infested offices and along with that a frequent fellow-query: "What comapany do you represent?" As though one could not merely represent oneself.

"I do not," I replied coolly, "have a card," and hung up.

After some sober thought, however, I am about to acquire my first business card while other plans gestate. I must say the idea begins to excite me. It will prove, along with any chance news item concerning myself, that I am alive, literally identifying me as lifelike. It shall have my name and address and phone number in the appropriate places, and in the upper corner, where a business identification is usually stated, there will mine appear. I decided to include the carefully chosen word: Systems. The technical nuance of that word "systems" will give instant assurance that the bearer of the card is no dreamy bumbler. It fits in with the technological ring of the times. As we know, there are no longer brakes or wheels on cars, but a car has a "braking system" or a "steering system." We have a land littered with hi-fi systems, weapons systems, energy systems, and a women's magazine recently introduced a new douche system. I foresee art systems, musical systems, and why not pornographic systems?

So be it.

817-664-1289	Poetry Systems
	Norman Rosten
by appt. only	

Max

As far as I was concerned (before it got complicated) I had a cashmere jacket that never fit properly, and Max was a tailor recently moved into the neighborhood. I had noticed him these past months sitting in a corner behind the plate glass of the cleaning store, completely visible to those passing by, bent over his machine or working with needle and thread. Normally tailors, an endangered species, would be out of sight, in the rear of such establishments; Max was rather saucily perched in his corner, as though he belonged there and nowhere else.

I thought that letting out the seam down the back of the jacket would give me more room. Max thought no, the problem was in the shoulders. It would be a bit more complicated. "And a bit more expensive," I said.

"Not too expensive, but right. It must be right. I have to cut at the shoulder, and sew back. Like a surgeon, he cuts away an arm or a leg, if he don't sew back just right, it's no good. It's the same thing with a suit. A surgeon can lose his patient, I can lose a customer, it's the same thing."

Although I liked the surgeon image, and his broken accent, I didn't think it was the same thing, and I was beginning to figure Max as a charming con man, I being the easily conned type.

"What will you charge me for the job?"

"Not too much."

"Because it's an old jacket and I don't want to pay you more for an alteration than the thing is worth."

"It must be perfect, I wouldn't let you go otherwise. Leave the jacket. Don't worry."

I didn't worry until I returned later in the week and tried it on. Something was wrong, and his eye caught it at once.

"My friend, one of your shoulders, excuse me, isn't right. It falls away, I can't explain it. Leave the jacket. Don't worry."

Actually, the problem was minor, and I said I'd take the jacket as is. "No," Max insisted. "A surgeon does not let a shoulder go out unless it fits right." He grinned, you had to like the man. "I can tell you, it's easier to be a doctor than a good tailor. I could be twice a doctor with all the work I do on fittings, alterations, everything. Because to lose a customer is like losing a life."

Put that way, I knew I had to come back. "By the way, I think the buttons are too small. Can you replace them?"

"To me, they seem fine—but whatever you say."

A week went by. I picked up the jacket, it looked and fitted right this time, except I had to struggle with the buttons. They were now a bit too large for the buttonholes. Max noticed my unhappiness.

"I'll change the buttons."

"I'm sorry I asked you to bother with these large ones. That was my mistake."

"Yes. But we can fix it. It must be right. I wouldn't let you go otherwise."

"What's the bill?" I asked, ready to flinch.

"When you come back after I fix the buttons," he answered. "Not much. I told you not much."

He was right. It wasn't much, but, I thought, five dollars wasn't enough either. I offered ten, he insisted on five, explaining that I had not pressed for quick service and therefore he had done the work at odd hours when things were slow.

"Max," I said, allowing my first touch of familiarity, "you're a character, almost a Brooklyn character."

He nodded gaily. "Yes, it's true, why not? You, too, could be a character."

"Thank you, Max."

"What is your work?"

"I'm a writer."

His eyes opened wider. "Books?"

"Books, yes. Sometimes." Then, the trap of vanity opened, I fell headlong in. "Matter of fact, I wrote a story once about a tailor. It's part of a longer story, a novel, about a boy who remembers his childhood, and how he delivered suits for a tailor. I'll drop off a copy."

Many days, perhaps a week, passed before I looked in again on my new friend (no escaping it) Max. He thrust aside a garment he was sewing, leaped up from his chair, reached across a work table, and grasped my arms. "Your book, I read it. All of it. Gorki! The people in the book, very good. Yes Gorki!"

That Max had read my entire book—I had merely marked the tailor sequence for him—was a surprise, but that he knew the name Gorki astonished me. While I would have felt giddy to be linked with Chekhov even in the faintest manner, I didn't feel slighted in the least with Gorki.

"You know Gorki?" I asked.

"Gorki, Chekhov, Gogol, Victor Hugo. I read all. I think Gogol—you know 'Dead Souls'?—too difficult. But beautiful. You agree?"

"Absolutely."

"Your stories good, all good. I enjoy everything you write. Bring me more." Then, briskly, businesslike, "The jacket is okay?"

"Okay, Max."

"Why don't you wear it?"

"I just don't wear it walking around."

"You wear it when you write?"

"No. When I go out on the town. It's my fancy jacket."

"The buttons are right?"

"Fine."

"It must be right. Come in again, we'll talk about the great writers. We talk about you, too." He grinned, he was an elf, small, puckish, bristling with energy.

Lunch followed some days later. Any man, or woman, who is wild enough to link me with Gorki is good for a lunch. During lunch, I inquired about his background. Max talked about Europe and his journey to America. A Polish Jew, he fled the Nazi invasion, was forced into a Russian labor camp for over a year and finally returned to Poland after the war. He became a designer of men's clothes and studied sculpture and drawing. In the mid-Fifties, bored with Poland and looking to expand his opportunities, he emigrated to the United States, meaning New York City, where he switched to designing women's clothes. It was stimulating, but chaotic. It fired an ambition in him to go into his own business, representing, at middle age, a final thrust for freedom. He would be his own boss.

"I walked around the streets, looking at stores, deciding on a location. Then I went into a store, this one, in the middle of the block, and asked the man if I could buy his business."

"You just walked in off the street?"

"Why not? I have a skill, a clothes surgeon, no? No! That's what the man said. But I liked the place, and the owner, and I said to him, 'You need a tailor, I can move in with my machine, there in the corner, and we can try.'"

"He didn't boot you out?"

"Why should he? Tailors don't grow on trees. I told him my experience, my background, he knows I can bring in business to him. We agreed. I moved in with my machine. I'm happy here. The people are nice, they appreciate good work. They tell me I'm the best."

"You are, Max. Expecially with buttons."

He nodded. "I know garments, arms, legs, coats, models, manikins, dresses, and always to fit right. I'm happy with my small machine, easy to pick up and go, if necessary, somewhere else. In case . . . "

"Even here?" I was surprised at the sudden yet casual turn in the conversation.

"Here, I don't think so." He winked, elf on a toadstool. "But the world is always a surprise. Always. That's why I like my machine, I carry it in, I can carry it out again. Let met tell you, my friend"—here he grew serious, even bitter—"when I was in Europe, in 1956, I was in Vienna waiting to come here to America. And friends came to Vienna, coming from Budapest when the Russians marched in with their guns. And who did the world love then? The Hungarian Freedom Fighters. But these fighters were going into the buildings in Budapest and putting a mark on the apartment doors of Jews. For what? For the German Nazis? For themselves? Who knows? I want to tell you, such Freedom Fighters you can keep. It is safer here. There are too many other things to do for Americans, I think they are too busy to hurt others." He grinned. "It's good to be busy."

"It's good to have a machine you can carry, too."

"You have a typewriter. You can carry it with you also, in a house, out of a house." It seemed to him the highest wisdom, to travel light and enjoy the work.

"I'll let you use my typewriter, Max. Time for you to write your book."

"Too late." He was firm. "One Gorki in this neighborhood is enough."

Why not? as Max would say. I never asked for praise. I just brought in a jacket for repair.

The Handball Connection

I have been involved most of my life in two important activities: handball and poetry. Handball came to me first, growing up in Coney Island, mecca of outdoor sports and sunshine. Poetry came to me later from those careless gods who might just as easily have turned me into a happy accountant. Though I was good at handball, poetry was my secret pride; yet the better I got as a poet, the more people told me what a jazzy handball player I had become. I brooded over this fate.

People understand the need to write poetry because so many write it so badly. But the mystique of handball puzzles or intimidates them. In an era of Big Bucks football, tennis, hockey, baseball with multimillion dollar contracts and the like, where does lowly handball fit in? It doesn't. It is not an Industry but rather the last (or close to last) of the innocent sports. It is played mostly outdoors, wherever one finds firm footing (concrete or wood) and a wall. It has no age limitation; from youth onward (lots of players in their sixties and seventies) till death do they part, player and wall. Comes spring, the sound of the handball is heard throughout the land. On the busier courts at Brighton Beach, Coney Island, or Brownsville—all Brooklyn Byzantiums—sideline betting goes on, but it's small stuff. It is still the test of small combats, single to single, twosome to twosome, striking that hard, dangerous, small black ball; gladiators in leather gloves. Lately, in the past two decades, the ball softened and came in more festive colors (blue, green, pink), the gloves replaced by wooden or metal paddles, easements scorned by the older veterans. More recently, women players have been appearing on the courts, at first to the consternation of the men; but soon admiration took over, for athletes respect the skill of competitors, and the women came on to win.

As handball historian and player Matthew Paris analyzes it: "These courts were the last big enclave of the game of immigrants. At the turn of the century the children of peasants in shapeless cloth that made them almost indistinguishable from small-town European landscapes hit the gray streets with stumpy hands distorted from childhood work and took out their masochism and fury on a hard black ball tough enough to break, bruise and tear at their fingers...." Now, from old dinosaurs such as these to the new generations of upwardly mobile young professionals, or the tough new ethnic influx, black or immigrant, they can be seen on the courts on goodweather days. But inclement weather does not deter: I have been ready in light rain and more than once have showed up with the snow half a foot or deeper on the court, and cleared away by four obvious madmen using shovels brought for the task.

Handball as poetry, why not? As much as the ancient discus or javelin of those early Greek athletes in their Olympic Games, celebrated by the poet Pindar. And now, handball, celebrated two thousand years later in the same short-line language.

> His fate is hard and black,
> a ricochet as fast
> as light that splits the line
> and gains the point.
> The ball
> is vengeance, his gloved hand
> drives it to the corner
> where it's curved, hangs
> for a lucky out.
> He stops,
> breathing hard and waits
> for a serve then fires
> a bullet with a spinning
> wrist that hugs the line
> and skips to the left.
> Point
> is his, grips the ball,
> skips it next to the right,
> the wall responding,
> and the city's hurrah
> that loves a Sunday winner!

Hair

My local barber is not very happy these days over the state of my hair. It is not being cut as regularly as he would like. Nor is there respect for style. The kids began something and the grownups caught the fever.

His philosophic rumblings came to the surface when we met at a traffic light recently. He asked whether I had been away on a trip. I lied and said yes. "Your latest haircut isn't too bad," he chuckled. "In fact, it kind of suits you. Where'd you get it, Chicago?"

I looked him directly in the eye. "I got it in my living room. My wife did it."

The light turned green, but he didn't move. Instead, he leaned against the traffic stanchion, his lips trembled. "Your wife?"

"What can I do, Peter? She likes to cut my hair."

"Yeah, but I'm your barber."

"You said yourself it looked good. Come on, I'll buy you a coffee."

Once settled, Peter remarked, "It's terrible, this whole thing going on about hair. I got nothing against you wife, I'm sure she's a lovely woman, but ..." he hesitated, shaking his head while looking at mine. "How'd she do it so good?"

It was time for man-to-man confidence. "I don't know and she doesn't know, Peter. It's the truth."

"What do you mean?" he asked shakily.

"She just cuts my hair. Without rhyme or reason. She just says to me one morning, whatever morning seems right for her, she says, 'Let me do it.'"

He sighed. "And you let her?"

I sighed in sympathy. "At first I thought it was a whim. To my surprise, she managed quite well. I mean, it made sense, what she did with the scissors. Although, just between you and me, I don't think she knows what she's doing. Except when I walk down the street, people compliment me on my haircut."

He dropped three additional spoons of sugar into his coffee—that made five. "The whole thing about hair today, it's ruining the country. The truth is"—he leaned forward confidentially—"there's no such thing anymore as a bad haircut. People will accept anything. They don't care. The guy on the street don't care, he's seen too many freaks to care. Out in the street anything goes. As a result, I get careless, I don't work with my usual skill. If it's too skillfull, they're not happy. Give it to 'em sloppy and they smile. You understand what that means?"

"What?" I asked politely.

"It means the end of an era. It means anybody can do it. Once anybody can barber, it's the end of barbering. The mystique is gone. Kids do it. Wives do it. I'll go out of business."

I nodded sympathetically. "Maybe it's just a fad."

"No," he continued grimly. "Once a woman finds out she can do something she enjoys, she won't give it up. Your wife, for instance. She likes to cut your hair, right?"

"Right."

"She won't stop. It's her pride. And she feels useful. And you enjoy it too. All that close attention, breathing down your neck. Be honest." He gulped the remaining coffee. "Amazing. You say she just sits you down at a mirror and starts cutting?"

"That's right."

"Do you tell her what to do?"

"I just say it looks nice, and she purrs like a cat and keeps going. The most interesting thing is the way she stops."

"How does she stop?" asked Peter, nervously.

"She just stops. Without any reason. As though she knows it's time to stop. Even when one sideburn is a bit longer than the other. Even when the back of the neck is uneven, or the hair is lumpy. But when I comb it out, and wash it, and walk down the street, people ask me, 'Who's your barber?'"

Peter moaned lightly. "It's scary, this whole thing. I hope you don't tell people your wife is your barber."

"No, I tell them you are."

He smiled wanly. "So I've lost a customer, eh?"

I replied, "She'll get tired of it. I'll come by again."

He got up. "Don't have to wait that long. Drop by anyway. Just to say hello and gossip." He waved to me as we parted but I could see he was an unhappy man.

A Tale of Two Precincts, Etc.

While I live in Police Precinct X, my stolen car was found in Precinct Y. It began as a typical city steal: the space in which I parked my car one evening contained, the next morning, another vehicle bearing no resemblance whatever to mine. Was I on the right street? The right side of the street? The right city? My lithe but battered four-wheeler was gone, I thought, at that moment already in a junkyard, the plates destroyed, stripped to the bare motor number. Perhaps a blessing in disguise. Parking is an urban curse. Those who like myself have stood bewildered on a windy corner trying to remember the spot where his car was last deposited will know what I mean.

Well, it was done. I reported the missing car in person at Precinct X, where, I was told, it would be put on the alarm. "What are my chances?" I asked a bored clerk. "Hundreds of cars are missing daily," she replied, with a wink. After a brief period of mild depression—an old car is, after all, an old friend—the absence of city parking responsibilities left me exhilarated. No more haunted dreams of Monday–Thursday versus Tuesday–Friday, and was I on the right side on Wednesday? I had slipped through the urban net.

Days passed, a week, two then three weeks, and no sign or word about my car. Gone to the graveyard. Gone to nuts and bolts, spare parts, the ultimate disgrace. Gone, the master brake cylinder; gone, the rebuilt starter, the new radiator core. The image of my car receded, grew fainter, and the morning came when I no longer saw myself as a car owner. I decided to wait one more week, after which I would cancel my insurance.

One evening several days later, I received a phone call. A man, speaking with a heavy accent (was it a friend playing a joke?), asked if I were the man who had lost a car. He went on to say there was a car on the street in front of his house, parked at an angle, for many days now. He had opened the door, which was unlocked, and in the glove compartment had found an old repair bill with my name on it. He then checked my number in the phone book, and sounded very pleased.

"It's your car, then?" he asked.

"Yes. Are the license plates on it?"

"Yes. Also, the wheels, the roof, everything. Even a parking ticket."

I blessed all the ethnics. I blessed the god of Lost and Found. I could not wait for the next day but journeyed at once to the far end of Brooklyn, walked several dark blocks past the subway, and there, parked badly at an angle, was my vehicle. I approached and looked inside. All seemed to be in order except that the ignition assembly on the wheel post had been skillfully removed. I longed to hear the purring of the motor, but that would have to wait for a mechanic next day. Meanwhile, the horn responded; and when the lights flicked on, my heart raced. It was alive! My dear departed, returned again to the living!

I went in to the house of my citizen benefactor and thanked him for phoning me. He reported that he had first called the local police precinct, but they would not come to check the car out, advising him instead to arrange for a tow truck to deliver it directly to the owner (me). This came as a shock. I had thought, in my naivete, that the police would look for abandoned and possibly stolen vehicles on the city streets.

Still, I was grateful to have my car back, miraculously unharmed and unvandalized. The next morning, ignition repaired, I became a daring driver again, avoiding potholes, drunken drivers, and crazy pedestrians. I thought the car ran even better than when I had last parked it, happy I suppose in the way rubber and steel can be happy when reunited with flesh and bones. We were together again, the sun was shining in Brooklyn, as I drove the long diagonal across the borough to my home precinct where I had first reported the car stolen over a month ago.

Inside the station house, I said to the woman clerk, "I'm here to report the recovery of a stolen car."

"When did this happen and where, honey?"

"Uh . . . I guess today, in Precinct Y."

"Was it stolen there?"

"It was stolen here a month ago, in this precinct, and recovered there."

"Well, you'll just have to go back and report it there. It's the law."

"But I live a couple of streets from here—"

She stirred in here chair impatiently. "Where is your car now?"

"Parked outside."

Her eyebrows—if that's what they were—raised an inch. "Did you drive your car here?"

"I sure didn't push it."

"Well," she said grimly, "you shouldn't be driving it nohow. It's on the alarm as a stolen car."

"But I'm the owner. Can't you un-alarm it?"

"I'm sorry, but you'll have to go back to the other precinct for that."

"I'm on my way." I didn't sound happy and I wasn't.

"You can't drive that car, mister!"

But I was out the door and into my stolen car that was no longer stolen. I drove away, retracing those long miles back across town to the Precinct Y headquarters where I explained my situation to another clerk, more beautiful and helpful.

She sighed. "You needn't have rushed all the way here for this. It's just a formality, a release form. We could have handled it over the phone."

"Your look-alike said it was the law."

She laughed merrily. "I suppose, but nobody's perfect, wouldn't you agree?"

"Let's get it over with," I said sullenly.

She sighed again. "They just don't think sometimes. I'll type these right up." After the papers were properly filled out registering the car as "recovered," she asked idly, "Where is your car now?"

"Outside," I said bluntly.

"Are you planning to use it?"

"I plan to drive home, which is way over on the other side of Brooklyn, where I just came from."

She rose, "I'm putting this right on the wire to cancel the alarm. It'll take about an hour to clear. Until then, you have to understand that your car is hot." She spoke firmly.

"Be reasonable," I said in what I considered my most reasonable voice. "If the owner is caught with his own stolen car, and your receipt of 'recovery' on his person—"

"Of course, if they pick you up . . . " she added nervously.

"Look, my dear," I believe I hissed, "they didn't pick up the car in a month, not even when they were invited to do so by the man who spotted it."

Now she was moving from her chair. "I'll put it on the wire. I'm only telling you the law."

I was out the door again, into my own car, and away with the vroom of a Triumph XZR-10. I roared across dear Brooklyn again, weaving recklessly in and out of traffic, hoping I'd be stopped by the police if only to announce I was driving a stolen car. But nobody stopped me. For all I know I may still be on the alarm, lost in the computer circuits, a menace to a sane society. And I like it that way as the weeks go by. I imagine when I'm stopped (it has to happen) by a police car, the rotating lights going, and the officer, gun drawn, advancing toward me, will shout, "Come on out with your hands over your head, and don't try anything funny." I get out of the car and turn to him with a cool and careful smile . . . .

The fates do not wish me well in the matter of car theft. On a bright carefree other morning I am in a friend's Cadillac borrowed from his Brooklyn garage so that I might drive my teenage daughter across the G.W. Bridge into New Jersey where she hoped to buy some "terrific" shoes at a "fabulous" warehouse sale. At the garage, the attendant nodded as I headed directly for the Cadillac which I had borrowed on a number of previous occasions. It was parked in a far dim corner. The key was in the ignition as usual. The car started and I waved to the attendant as I drove away; before long I picked up my daughter and headed north. The car, a light tan, seemed dirtier than I ever recalled seeing it; however, the interior, usually messy, was neatly vacuumed, which struck me as odd. I would have to point this out to David, the owner, just to see if there was a laugh in it somewhere.

To thank him for the use of the car, I stopped at a gas station to fill the tank. It was then I first noticed the Florida license plates. He had visited Florida the past winter and spoke of moving there later on; he may have gotten the plates on his visit. This was his car, down to the cigarette lighter, I reassured myself.

Across the beautiful bridge into Jersey (dull steel compared to the eloquent stone of my Brooklyn span) and on to a nearby town and the "stupendous" shoe sale. While my daughter giddily shopped, I parked the car and read a magazine. Then I decided to call home; being so far from Brooklyn always induces anxiety.

"Hello," I said into the phone.

My wife answered. "Where are you?"

"I'm in New Jersey."

"Well, turn right around and get back to David's garage as soon as you can."

My throat constricted. "What happened?"

"You took the wrong car. The police are after you. Call the garage. Hurry!"

I called the garage. "Listen, I borrowed the Cadillac and I phoned home—"

"Are you Norman? This is Harry. Have you been drinking? You drove away with the wrong Cadillac."

"But it's the same Cadillac I often borrow from Schuman—"

"It's a darker brown."

"Slightly darker, Harry—"

Harry exploded. "It wasn't green or pink, was it? And with a Florida license plate, are you blind?"

"It looked pretty much like the other one. Admit it."

Harry quieted down. "Okay, I admit it. But the owner's screaming."

"Can't the owner use that other Cadillac meanwhile?"

"He wants his own fuckin' Cadillac. He's from Florida. He hates New Yorkers. Bring it back pronto."

"On my way."

"He reported it, against my advice. It's on the police alarm. If you're stopped, I dunno . . . recite a poem. Good luck!"

Roaring through traffic, a hunted man again, police cars passing me with traffic everywhere, I'm wondering what to do if the siren starts going. I'm on the police wire again, the high wire, doing my act, the rotary brushes whirling and me hurrying back from...Jesus, New Jersey!

How did I get here?

View From
Beneath the Bridge

There are days when the Brooklyn Bridge, half-shrouded in mist, seems an apparition, a Japanese print, a foundering supertanker. Then there are clear days when it looms as a geometric miracle; on such days the structure invites the walker into its steel web, and I often accept the invitation; one never gets enough of this mystery and exhilaration.

At the Brooklyn end of the Bridge (I rarely bother with the Manhattan side, though I know it exists), one may visit a small restaurant/bar, called Harbor View, owned by my friend Phil. He has the rugged look of a longshoreman, tough, muscular, yet he runs an establishment of a certain elegance, uniformed waiters with French or Italian accents, sometimes a singer or pianist. The tables and furnishings are imitation Versailles. And an entire side of the building, all glass doors, faces out upon the East River and, directly overhead, the great Bridge.

It was, for many years, the only restaurant in that area. When a new and flashier establishment opened directly at the riveredge, adjacent to the Bridge and a hundred yards from a cultural point called BargeMusic, the Beautiful (meaning wealthy) People descended in long and heavy cars to fill it with dinner parties. This influx of the Manhattan slumming parties (wow! look at that Bridge!) did not disturb Phil. New money did not excite him, he had the loyalty of old friends. The friends gave off the ambience of discredited politicians, retired jockeys, uptown bouncers, and possibly vice-presidents of banks. Phil would move around the tables, greeting people, bringing the wines, making the place hospitable. He would often join a table and a meal in progress, as if he were a late arrival in the party. Jacket off, tie loose, he looked ready for an old-fashioned poker game.

Some years back, I dropped in for a beer after a concert at the Barge. I asked a gentleman at the bar, not knowing he was the proprietor, if I could use a table next to the open doors. He nodded. I sat down and lifted a glass to the spirit of Hart Crane, an earlier Bridge poet. I returned several days later and had another. Introducing himself, Phil joined me.

"You like that Bridge?" he asked jovially.

"The best."

"You come from the other side?" (He meant Manhattan.)

"No, I live near here, up the hill."

"Funny about alla people come just to look up at it. Like it was some monument."

"Well, it is. A monument that people use every day, walking to work, driving across—"

He interrupted with a chuckle, "And once in a while jumping off, heh?" He brushed some crumbs from the table. "You know that lady Olga Bloom who runs the Barge? Terrific lady."

"She's a friend."

"Bring her by for a drink, on the house, my pleasure. Includes you. So you're a musician there, must be, right?"

"No. I'm just a man about town, sort of. How long you been with this place?"

"Five six years maybe. Come any time you like, you don't have to buy a beer, just come sit and look at the Bridge any time you like. If you're Olga's friend, that's your ticket."

"Thanks, I'll do that."

"I see you write things in a little book. Are you from a newspaper?"

Well, I was cornered, and no harm in confession. "Just scribbling stuff for myself. I'm a writer."

"That's what the cop said who wuz writing out a parking ticket." He laughed loudly at this show of humor. "Listen, if you want to bring a typewriter and type your book lookin' up at the Bridge—"

"No, thank you. I don't always use a typewriter. You know, in the real old days, writers used a quill, a goose feather. The stem is hollow, they make a cut at the bottom and dip it in a bottle of ink and it holds the ink, then you write like it's a pen, except it isn't."

He asked, "What about the feather part?"

"You don't use it, it just looks good. Before the fountain pen or ball point, the quill was what you used."

Phil shook his head, intrigued. "So what do you write?"

"Poetry, also a lot of checks."

"Hey, who don't write checks? But I never known any grown men who write poetry. And you was born here?" Now his interest became more serious. In this jungle, under his very nose, a poet with a quill which he could probably use if there were no more typewriters. This was something new.

"Since we're friends," I volunteered, "I wrote a poem to the Bridge last year for the centennial celebration. The official poem."

"You wrote it?"

"I also read it under the Bridge, in a boat of course, that night with all the fireworks, remember? A hundred boats at least."

"Are you kidding" he responded excitedly. "Two, three hundred counting the little ones. Musta been hundreds of empty booze bottles floating in the harbor. And maybe some bodies too. My place was jumpin'. They should have a centennial every ten years, why not?"

"Because every ten years isn't a hundred."

"So listen, you got a book with your poems?"

"Not on me."

"I mean in a store, can I buy it? Here, write down the name, I'll buy it and next time you drop by you can autograph it. I'd like that, show to my customers. Because I never met a poet. I'd be proud to show you off." His enthusiasm was genuine, not literary. I guessed he was not a book person, I guessed about a book a year. But he totally demolished that cliche of awed reader meeting the writer; it was to him an easy event, and to me a pleasure.

Weeks later, following a concert at the Barge, I dropped in at the Harbor View. Phil saw me enter, he waved and dashed into the kitchen, then returned in a moment holding a copy of my book aloft, grinning excitedly. The place was almost empty. He called out, "I have it, your book, beautiful picture on the front, hey where'd you get that picture, you look like a longshoreman. I like that picture!"

I wondered if he had got past the picture into the book, but said nothing. He led me to my favorite table, we sat down, and he opened the book, riffling the pages as though it were a deck of cards. "I looked in the pages, and read a little bit." He was suddenly sheepish. "It's a good thing you had a typewriter when you wrote all that stuff. The quill woulda taken years." And he laughed.

"I'm glad you liked some of it."

"I keep it here and show it to the customers. I tell them you're one of my customers. I want you to write something good when you autograph it."

"How about 'To Phil, a good friend in a friendly restaurant?'" Before he could reply, I wrote the inscription and my name. And added, "Under the Brooklyn Bridge."

He read it and marveled. He shook my hand. "How about a drink? Both of us." He signaled to a waiter, then he lowered his voice. "I looked through the book but didn't see that thing you wrote about the Bridge."

"It's not in the book."

"Not in the book?" Alarm was in his voice. "Why not?"

"It isn't published yet. I wrote it after the book came out. Maybe in my next book."

"You mean it ain't here? Why couldn't you put it in?"

"Well . . ." I could see he was clearly perplexed. "The book was done. You can't just stick in an extra page."

"Where is the poem? I like that idea of a poem about the Bridge," he said doggedly.

"I have it at home. I'll drop off a copy."

"But I want it in the book which I show to my friends. The whole idea, y'see, with my place here under the Bridge and it ain't in the book." I regarded him helplessly, sophisticated man vs. noble savage. Then his face broke out into a smile. "Tell you what, could you write the poem in the book? There's some empty pages in the back. I'd appreciate it."

He apparently could not see the poem existing outside the book. The book was reality. I said, "I could do that, but it's not like a printed page, you understand."

"If it's in the book, fine. That's where I want it. You take it home and write it in then drop if off later."

And so, on the last endpaper of my book, in the only copy extant, in a small handwriting, are the lines of a poem entitled "Brooklyn Bridge" which Phil shows to his customers as proof positive that I exist.

Brooklyn Bridge

It stands above a century of winds,
colossus anchored in tides,
still surprising the landscape.

Light upon the cables,
weight gathered within
The stone towers: a tension
spooled out as steel,
now compacted into giant shoulders.
On some days a lithograph,
on others a choir of strings,
our Gothic incarnation;
finally, a curve of silence
upholding a world, as Roebling dreamed . . .

The dream to reach beyond structure,
arrive at a waiting future:
and it is here.
                    Aloof to the age,
its beauty and line intact,
we see again the pink-veined stone
flowering to the arch, holding
the strands of cable woven by
forgotten fingers. The city flows
to the horizon, heavy with smoke
and the death of architecture,
yet the Bridge will soar, and sing,
rising with dawns and mists,
poised for another leap of time.

Wheels accelerate on the span,
rasping like wasps in their madness,
drone of the living and the dead.
The century, begun on these cobbles,
turns on that weightless arc,
turns with the sun, with light,
as ghosts of the sailing ships
ride the same harbor.

The Last of
the Brooklyn Spacemen

The voice on the phone was very polite. "Good morning, sir. Are you the owner of an automobile, license number XK7041?" It was 8 AM, a dreaded hour. I was barely awake. Was my car stolen? Or illegally parked? Or used in a crime? I mumbled a cautious reply, "It may possibly be my car. I'll check that license."

The male voice went on, "We have already checked, sir. This is Con Edison, Service Maintenance. Would you be kind enough to move your car? You are parked over our manhole." I stared dumbly into the mirror behind the phone, receiver against my ear. "We are holding a space for you."

Was I dreaming? Such charm, such politeness! Or was it a trick. I had recently written the company a threatening letter about air pollution. Were they holding my car as hostage?

My first thought was of one or more men trapped below the street, gasping for air, looking up from the manhole into the underside of my car. But that was impossible; the day was beginning, they couldn't have been down there all night.

"By the way, where is my car parked?"

"Joralemon, between Henry and Hicks."

"Give me ten minutes," I said.

I arrived at my car, just around the corner from my residence, to discover it jammed between two steel monsters, the fins of one in my radiator grille, and the grille of another locked in the bumper. The driver of a Con Ed truck was waiting in a shiny hardhat, amazingly wide awake. Directly across the street, outlined by markers, was my reserved space.

He waved a hand in friendly greeting. "We had this manhole roped off last night with markers. Kids probably stole 'em. Sorry to bother you. We appreciate your moving over."

"It's okay," I said. I started my car while he held up traffic to allow me to blast out, swing around, and back into the new space. The man said, "We figured as long as we found another spot, you wouldn't mind. Otherwise, we wouldn't ask you."

"Otherwise, I wouldn't have moved," I said flatly.

"Parking that bad here?"

"Murder," I replied. "Where you from?"

"Queens."

"How's it there?"

"Suicidal." And he returned to his work.

I watched him and another man lift the manhole cover, ring the opening with their yellow conical markers, and descend into the dark cavity of Underground Brooklyn. I patted my car, covered by a thick layer of city fallout and Con Ed talc, and surveyed the street. Wall to wall parking. Safe for the day, at least. Safe on a Monday–Thursday side, and here it was Tuesday. A two-day gift of the gods.

While I did not quite grow up in the era of the horse and buggy, I do recall a neighborhood where one thing was fairly constant: There was always a place to park. In this particular part of Brooklyn with its tree-lined streets and brownstone houses, one could, until recent years, boast a sense of seclusion from the world. There was no traffic problem. When the first NO PARKING signs went up, no one took them too seriously. A scattering of tickets gave us only a stoic scorn. We were not going to give up the right to park our cars in front of our own houses. Kids would snap off radio aerials, dogs would mistake our tires for trees, but we intended to enjoy squatters' rights.

The police continued to put up new signs. Simple alternate-side 8 TO 11 AM PARKING, then the NO PARKING 8 AM TO 6 PM were followed by the more formidable NO PARKING 8 AM TO MIDNIGHT then the NO STANDING NO PARKING ANY TIME ultimatum, but the spaces were yielded only grudgingly. Sneak police raids made little if any gains. Cars were quickly shuttled away, but just as quickly brought back a day later. Like all raids by cowardly men, they were not repeated too often in the same territory. And, in a time of full employment, a small parking fine can be endured.

I could understand better, as time went on, men's fierce attachment to land throughout history. Land was always . . . well, just land. Who needed it but landlords and farmers? But when I inherited my old vehicle and found a snug harbor in front of my house, I began to feel this hunger. It was, after all, only a ten- or fifteen-foot-strip of parking space, but it was enough. It was *belonging*. I knew then why peasants all over the world resisted collectivization. To the farmer his field, to the city man his parking space—so ran the new slogan in my head.

In this curious development—to which, I might add, very little attention has been given by sociologists—the owner of the parking space (whom I will refer to as a spaceman) began to grow sullen about the threat to his freedom to park. In the early stages, he had been carefree about riding through town and occasionally over pedestrians, bouncing off abutments and bridges, and bashing against windshields; now, as his domain became smaller, he became less adventurous. He began to guard his space; the idea of moving troubled him. What he would not say aloud, but obviously shone from this haunted eyes, was the question: *Will I lose my space?* Thus, plagued by every kind of anxiety, a still new one began to torment modern man.

Slowly the car owner, garageless specimen of the cities, refused to move his car. Why move? the saying went. Or, a car in a space is worth two on the road. Months (years?) passed. A film of dust and hydrocarbon stain settled upon the rows of parked cars. Street upon street of inert cars. On weekends, of course, the pressure became great. Wives would force husbands to get in and at least drive around the block, but this often turned out to be a harrowing experience. Landless cars from other boroughs, lurking on the avenues, would dash in and grab a space the instant it was vacated. Many a man roamed these streets for hours, trying to get back his old space. But alas, poaching was the order of the day—and night. You left your space at your own peril.

Most of us stayed put. Those who dared to turn on the ignition key numbered a small desperate minority. Most of us were content to wait it out. Society had made spacemen of us, and spacemen we would remain. On sunny days along our streets, families sat near their parked cars, or puttered around them cleaning the windshield or dusting the hood. A few washed the tires. Here and there, a motor would turn over, sputter and race. Dozens of heads would look up and smile. Ah, the call of the open road!

Those with new cars suffered more acutely than others. I, for example, had an old car, unpolished, beginning to rust; long trips were quite out of the question for its fading range. I was content to be a spaceman. But those who had to keep all the modern horsepower in check were the true sufferers.

I was the first to sell my battery. I reasoned, quite simply, why a battery if I'm never going anywhere? Meanwhile rumors were constantly reaching us about new developments elsewhere. We knew about the police drive over the Bridge, where cars were given no mercy—a development known as "Tow-Away Zone." Cars were being towed away at an astonishing clip. Very often with people in them. Tow-trucks hungrily toured the streets fighting for victims, and woe to the errant spaceman caught there. To further complicate matters, some tow trucks were dropping cars in the rivers at either side of the city. Many a sundown saw a bottleneck of cars drifting down the Narrows out to sea. It was, as one columnist put it, plain murder. There, in Manhattan, a commercial stronghold, things naturally had to be tough. Here, we reasoned, in Brooklyn, a relatively pastoral community, the need for theatrics was hardly necessary.

The first "Tow-Away" sign hit our area like a thunderclap. We had suffered the intrusion of Parking Meters, and more menacing, confusing signs, but this was war. A rush on batteries and tires (some had jacked up rear ends and disposed of rear tires) quickly brought the vehicles up to Operational Strength. There was a period of tuning up of motors. We knew that the police always allowed several days for the signs to sink into the consciousness of potential violators. But, as the hours ticked by, a feeling of hopelessness crept into the ranks. Not a free street remained. Free people without free streets.

We had reached the point where men eyed one another furtively from behind curtained windows. Lights burned far into the night. What was each man thinking about in this democracy? Not his neighbor's wife, but his neighbor's space. The police, no doubt guided by sadistic psychiatrists, had played a diabolical hand. They had cleverly set one half of the street against the other. Neighbor against neighbor. Monday-Wednesday-Friday against Tuesday-Thursday-Saturday. It left Sunday free, a cheap sop to our conscience.

I shall never forget that first 8 AM when the Monday Men lined up at their cars, started up the motors with a roar, and shamefacedly drove off. In their houses, the Tuesday Men knew the game was up. They had but one more day. At first, many of them would cruise around from eight to eleven, hoping to get back to their still-warm places. But it didn't work. The streets were full of vagrants who, having heard of the situation, knew just how to take advantage of it. These bully outsiders would get the vacant spaces at ten-thirty, sit out the remaining minutes, lock their cars and dash away. The Monday Men would often cruise the streets on Monday nights, hoping a tired Tuesday man would vacate the night before, which sometimes happened. An incredible chaos developed. Blood often flowed a few minutes to eleven o'clock when hundreds of cars (some driven by the wives of the men who had left for work) dived for the empty spaces. But it was always the same: the happy few hooted at by their spaceless neighbors.

Actually, it could not have ended otherwise. A government study suggested there was no way to beat the game. A majority of cars would be doomed, like dead satellites, to circle their streets in regular orbits.

I am luckier than some of my fellow citizens. Having my own hours, with few if any morning appointments, I can leisurely move my car from one side of the street to another, or cruise about at will, until I pick up a choice space. It means getting up earlier, but even this has had compensations. I have gotten to know the new bearded street cleaner, the mailman, my super, and have a nodding acquaintance with several women on the block who pass me, fragrant with perfume, on their way to the subway.

I have witnessed many battles in the war between the police department and the garageless motorist. Most recently there has been an attempt to simplify things. New green signs tell of PARKING PERMITTED MON & THURS (or TUES & FRI) 8 AM TO 6 PM ONLY with NO PARKING OTHER TIMES in red underneath. I'm sure the drawing boards are hot with even newer ideas, but I have no doubt that recent emigration from the borough can be traced directly to this blundering bit of civic planning.

The Olga Affair

I'm not ashamed to talk about it. I fell in love with a lady who owns a barge. Did we meet madly on this barge which is moored under (almost) the Brooklyn Bridge and make love with the tugs racing by and the skyscraper lights winking at us? Or dance across the glorious polished floor? Of course not. This isn't a movie; it's real life; what's more, it's Brooklyn real life which in mathematical terms is life squared.

I think of it as *l'affaire du pont*. Because maybe without the Bridge it wouldn't quite have the passion. Yet I feel should the Bridge vanish I'd still basically feel the same about Olga. Can a poet and barge-person find happiness in the twentieth century? These are questions, again, which neither of us explores. We have the Bridge which we share along with chamber music. That is enough.

Our relationship covers barely half a dozen years. It began at a time when Olga was struggling to bring forth her plan that came to be known as BargeMusic. Music on a barge, moored to a spit of real estate called Fulton Ferry Landing. How did this now successful venture come about? It may one day be said, as is the way with myths, that Olga stood on the banks of the East River, just south of the Brooklyn Bridge, and lassoed a derelict barge as it floated by. And she might very well have done so. Yet the facts are just as intriguing. It begins with her statement, not very elegant but to the point: "I hocked my house and bought a barge."

Olga is a pianist and violinist, perhaps not of concert caliber, but she knows a bow from an arpeggio, and has the inborn spirit of the artist. Her dream of a home for chamber music probably had its origin in her genes—how else to explain this peculiar kind of fanaticism? But the obstacles were formidable.

Olga's barge appeared doomed to float away its life in the hinterlands of Brooklyn. Her inquiries to find a mooring spot along the New York harbor piers got nowhere. The resistance was not malicious. It was ignorant: the people who ran the city had no idea of the laws governing the "cultural" use of pier space or any other space on the interborough waterways. There may very well have been no laws on the books. It seemed, from what I can make of Olga's history, that a friend, or friendly official, allowed her to use a mooring just south of the Bridge on the Brooklyn side of the East River. At first the city—again, through ignorance—raised a brouhaha about this ugly duckling suddenly afloat on the pristine (littered & polluted) waterfront. Who invited her to drop an anchor? And a woman! While it was being considered as to how to deal with Olga, she stayed put. "Bureaucratic indecision," she explained with some relish, "gave me the time to prove that the idea of music here was viable. It gave me some breathing space." The sound of the violins continued to be heard.

While ominous neighbors treated her with suspicion, the gods sent supporting messengers in the shape of angelic dockworkers who helped her get the barge into shape to pass various city inspections. These new friends installed safety items, rewired when needed, regarding the musical instruments with awe as they worked. Word got out, other volunteers showed up and pitched in, an Irish postal worker, Italian passerby, and others, with Red Noto, the loyal longshoreman, keeping a general lookout for city inspectors or hooligans. They liked Olga and were determined to see that she stayed. Somehow (which explains all improbable things) the authorities, faced with a *fait accompli*, accepted her. She was there, she was smart, and gathering support not only by her personality but the strains of Mozart, Schubert, and Ravel. Something new had blossomed in the neighborhood, no doubt about it; her name was Olga, and she was a charmer and a fighter.

Next she began to make the important corporate contacts: local banks, corporations such as Con Ed and Brooklyn Union Gas—all local establishments that she could get support from in various ways. Meanwhile, back at the Barge, concert attendance grew, the word spread, culture-hungry people from the Hill (the Heights) came down to see, and came again, and soon the place was a hit. As a musician, Olga knew how to get the best, mostly youthful players (occasionally she'd flash an old pro like Walter Trampler) and form them into an ensemble; it was pick-up stuff, but these were well-trained and professional, and soon absorbed the Barge spirit. A jolly time was had by all, with Olga as hostess, greeting the customers and sending them out again like the minister of a church.

These young artists took a chance. Their promising uptown careers could be jeopardized by appearing where they did (what's this? playing on a barge in Brooklyn?), but they came aboard with courage and verve. They challenged the bureaucracy. Musicians are traditionally loners. The barge gave them responsibility and a group spirit they rarely experienced in their young careers. Here they found an oasis where they could mix musical adventure with standard repertoire. Most important, they worked out the schedule—chamber music twice each week, year round—and chose who should play when and with whom, and chose the program. Musicians appearing with such prestigious groups as the Lincoln Center Chamber Society, and involved in world-wide competitions—they were now virtually in command. They understood how unique this experience was: use of the waterfront, exclusive chamber music, artistic control. This was musical nirvana: happiness in Brooklyn!

Olga was firm on calling the artists the true heroes in her struggle. "Not to forget," she quickly adds, "the other artists, writers, and poets who rallied to my side and stayed there. No summer soldiers in this army."

She seemed never to be free of the petty frustrations of an artist trying to perform her work. While the surroundings became more amenable, it was some time before the neighbors openly cheered. With the success of the outdoor River Cafe, a hundred yards to the north, Olga's Barge suited the new gentrification (upgrading for the upper class) of the area. Chic spread its commercial balm in this small area of warehouses and factories, some converted to co-op apartments. Over the Bridge from Manhattan came the Mercedes, BMW's, Cadillacs, and assorted limos, all carrying the Beautiful People to pockmarked Brooklyn, to taste of culture and good food in the shadow of Urban Renewal. River Cafe, Harbor View Restaurant, Roebling's Bridge—and BargeMusic!

The Barge itself, refurbished, varnished, scrubbed, in the beginning attracted thieves and petty delinquents. Break-ins occurred. Olga talked about one of these. "For about a week, a gang of young punks would get into the Barge at night, observed by a neighbor who reported to me. They seemed harmless, maybe the Barge was some kind of game. I thought if they behaved, I wouldn't report it. Once they used our typewriter and left crazy messages. They were heard playing the piano far into the night. Maybe they were chamber music buffs." She laughed, then her face hardened. "One night the little bastards stole a violin. It was luckily an old beat-up practice violin, but they just missed an expensive viola. Then I called in the cops. They picked the kids up, as usual they were soon released. Never saw the violin again. They came back while awaiting sentence, leaving things around, a sprig of leaves on the typewriter, music books open, fireplace used. Their behavior baffled me. I didn't know what they'd do next. Then I checked with my longshoreman friend Noto. He wanted to know what the kids were, Italian, Irish, Jewish. I knew from the police blotter they were Italian. Noto nodded and said, Leave it to me. And, you know, those kids never bothered me again. What a friend to have, this Noto!

"So here I am where I want to be, me and the Barge and the wonderful audiences who attend my concerts on Thursday and Sunday, with special concerts on Easter, Christmas, whenever. And not to mention—which I always do—those other community events such as parties, weddings, business lunches, bar mitzvahs, the works. And I continue to give music lessons to underprivileged kids. Culture is my base, but I have to keep an eye on profit and loss. I won't bore you with my operating expenses. I'm doing okay, I'm now in the black. But mostly I'm established here. I'm performing a service here. I love it, the people love it. And the sound of music is healthy for everyone."

Music on the Barge

Noah had his Ark,
Olga her Barge; putting
the context aside, the cargo, the flood,
we think her Barge the truer miracle,
and made of superior wood.

Upon the tide of indifference
Olga's smile caught the wind,
and music came aboard: strings
and flutes and drums, paired or not,
just so they were hot.

The waters raged, the instruments
did not panic; Olga exclaimed,
"It's only the waves, not to worry;
play; if lost, we can't drift
very far; New Jersey or Staten,
batten down the *scherzo*,
cometh the dove, lovely *adagio*,
finale ahead, land, land!"

We made it. Do you think
our human creatures are happier
to be saved? Applause, bravo,
and a new concert tomorrow!

Super-Octogenarian

The sound of a harpsichord drifted down the stairwell from an open door. Scarlatti? Bach? One of these, surely—though on some days there's Joplin—but only one man capable of playing them all. And yes, he built the thing himself (with parts already assembled, of course).

Bert is eighty-five, and while he doesn't bound up the stairs of his three-flight walkup—as I do my second—he manages well enough. Neighbors wondered for many weeks while various lumbers were delivered or hauled up the stairs to become . . . what? A bookcase? A table? Then, one day, he invited them in, whisked a cloth from off a miniature form, et viola, a harpsichord! Then, he brushed off a rickety chair, sat down and played a bit of Handel, smiling through the white beard that gave him a late-Whitman look. That same wise quizzical look, and the same cryptic wisdom if you could provoke him to speak: it was a wisdom that often showed itself as a question. For example, on the occasion when I read my poetry at a public gathering of souls, Bert was in the audience, and after the reading astonished all with the question: "Can the poet tell us in a few words, what is going to happen to all of us?"

Laughter. Applause. But some apprehension. It was not merely the nuclear shadow, but the shadow of mortality, that muffled the laughter. My reply was to recite two lines by a Spanish poet named Antonio Machado: "The spring has arrived/No one knows what happened." It was the meeting of two ambiguities—poetic truths, if you will—giving us a taste of truth. Only a taste, since pure truth, like pure oxygen, would likely be fatal.

Bert is the oldest resident in the brownstone, and the longest. He had been for many years (decades) a merchant seaman, lecturer and author on labor and radical movements of the twentieth century, once an officer of the American Recorder Society, and involved in local agitations such as rent strikes and anti-nuclear protests. He's slowed down a bit in body but hardly in spirit, though his prophecies (he has the prophet look) are less certain. His basic optimism about the human race is reflected on blustering wintry days when he can be seen bending into the wind, often wearing only a jacket. He rarely caught cold. He would say, "The germs have given up on me. They go for tender meat."

Our street's elder statesman, he would say, "If a bill collector should ask for me, tell him I've gone for a walk some weeks ago and haven't been heard from since." He'd often startle me at the window, looking into my room where I'd be at my desk, and sweetly ask, "Are you decomposing?" His quirks (what's a quirk but a sign of character?) set the tone for a once rebellious neighborhood. His landlord had been trying to lure Bert from his long rent-protected residency in a most valuable apartment, offering a cash bonus and a more modern apartment elsewhere if he'd leave quietly. Bert took just enough of the bait to see what was available, then turned down the offer. "It was tempting," he explained, "but I have my library to consider. There wouldn't be enough room in any of those new places for my thousand or more books. I don't intend to leave a lifetime of books behind for a clean elevator building full of condo people. Not my type. I'm a walkup type."

He was generally buoyant toward his fellow man, but could be touchy. A plumbing problem developed somewhere between his floor and mine; water began trickling along the hallway ceiling which I diagnosed as a pipe leaking between the floors. When the leak stopped, then started again, then stopped, the problem needed more than an amateur diagnosis; it needed a licensed plumber. One such fellow finally showed up with the threatening look all Brooklyn plumbers seem to have (it says, "Don't make trouble or I'll destroy the house"). I led the gentleman upstairs. Linda, Bert's sometime companion and longtime sub-tenant, opened the door and said, "He's in the bath. Could be forever."

I entered, plumber in tow. I knocked at the bathroom door. No opened the door. The plumber was right behind me with his bag of tools; he had a Pete Rose haircut so I liked him right away. What we saw was an elderly sharp-eyed bearded man seated in a half-filled bathtub calmly reading The New York Times.

"Yes?" He turned to us with an imperial look.

"We hate to bother you this way," I began. "This guy's a plumber—"

He cut in sharply, "You are bothering me, despite your explanation. A man's tub is his castle, may I remind you."

"Your water is dripping down my ceiling."

"How do you know it's my water? There's water all over this leaky ship. Can the plumber come back later?"

I said, "Let the guy check for leaks or whatever. Don't be a piece of floating blubber, okay?"

"I resent that," he replied, turning a page carefully.

I asked the plumber. "Can you come back later?"

"Not today I can't," replied Pete.

Now I was getting annoyed. "He won't bother you, Bert. He's going to poke around, so read on and be quiet."

Pete said, "I have to get to my truck for a special wrench. This tub is a coupla hundred years old."

I followed him out to the hall. He asked, "What's with him?"

"He's an octogenerian, you know, eighty plus, and a bit deaf and takes two, three baths a month. This is the day. Lovable guy really."

He nodded. "I'll be right back. Five minutes. Tell him he can get outa the tub while I'm gone if he's afraid I'm a peeping plumber."

I returned to the bathroom. "You want to get out? He'll be back in five minutes."

Bert was now at the editoral page. "I'm not rushing out for no plumber."

"What do you want?" I shouted. "He's here, stop being a prima donna. Let the man do his work."

"I'm not a prima donna. I'm in my bath with The New York Times and you people are intruding. But don't let me stop you. Old folks have to put up with this. He doesn't look like a plumber to me. More like the landlord on a slumming tour." He snorted obscenely and continued to read during the plumber's pipe inspection as though the man was not there.

The next morning he knocked on my door. I opened it and saw a chastened Bert, who entered timidly. "I hope the plumber plumbed correctly."

"Turned out to be something very minor. Come in."

"You'll notice I'm in already. Can you spare a few moments?"

"Take five. And relax, old boy."

He was unusually solemn as he sat down, and nervously stroked his expansive white beard. "I've got to get this problem settled once and for all. It's been going on too damn long."

I knew what the problem was, and waited for him to play his scene. "She's got to go!" he began with explosive emphasis. He was referring to Linda, the lady in his home. "I will not put up with it any longer. Why should I?" he added belligerently.

"You can't just put her out."

"Why can't I?" he sputtered. "I'm getting older and I need a quiet place to live. There's no quiet here. Her friends drop in any hour of day or night. They bring wine. They play their damn transistor radios past midnight. And her cats. You know those cats, three, four, ten for all I can tell the way those cats dash in and out of the window. And they pee everywhere. They pee on my bed when they get too lazy for their box, or want a change of venue. They are a menace. No, no, she can't stay on."

"Where will she go? Find her a place. Do you know of a place? It's hopeless in this city."

"I hold the lease!" he roared. "She's overstayed her welcome."

"Look, Bertie, you can't do it. She's a beautiful woman. She's not that old but old enough to need and appreciate a home, which is here. Don't be a tyrant."

He suddenly caved in, his voice muted. "I don't know how to tell her, it's the truth." Then, fiercely muttering, "But she's got to go."

"We'll all hate you. We'll hiss as you go by."

He cackled. "You'd do that? How about that!"

"Give it some thought, old buddy."

He paused, as though to let the idea sink in. "The truth is, I can't handle the situation, telling her to leave. I don't know how to tell her. But I deserve more peace than I'm getting. I'm old enough to have

But I deserve more peace than I'm getting. I'm old enough to have earned that."

"I agree. But she's here."

"Yes, and she's got to go!" He pounded the table as he rose, a reflex that soon passed into a more ruminative mood. "Imagine this trouble at my age. I'd see an analyst, but if you have no problems when you go in, you sure as hell will have some when you leave."

"Well," I said soothingly, "you do have a problem. Nothing wrong with a consultation. Go with an open mind."

"You give me your blessing?" He was trying to lighten the matter.

"I do, brother."

"The idea bothers me. But so does doing nothing." And he left.

He appeared subdued when I next saw him.

"How's it going, Bert?"

"I consulted a friend who told me I had unconscious hostility and for some time and money an analyst could beat it out of me." He smiled wryly. "I told him I couldn't afford a cure. Also, my hostility was completely conscious, so what does he know? Meanwhile, Linda and I are friendly again. She does have some good qualities, mind you. But I need my solitude."

"It'll be worse without her."

He spun around. "Why do you say that?"

"Because you'd fall apart alone."

He stared at me in disbelief. I had struck at the core of his ego. He looked crestfallen and being a softie I added, "And if you don't, she will."

"She will, eh?" That idea seemed to please him.

"The point is, you need one another."

He nodded, baffled. "I'll give her another six months to find a place. I don't want her friends to think I'm a total monster. But I very well may be. And I'm not going to pay a shrink to find out."

"Sleep on it."

"I've been doing that, friend." He laughed gleefully. "Nothing much else I can do with it. You see, with her in the apartment I can't bring up women easily. And you got to corner 'em before you try anything." He smiled sadly. "I'd have a fighting chance if I was alone." He thought about it for a moment, then shook his head as though to dispel a fantasy or challenge. "Well, time for an early nap. Then I'm off to a concert. Rudolph Serkin, great pianist. I'll get my usual VIP stage chair at Carnegie."

"How do you rate that, smart guy?"

He winked. "I go to the manager. I say I'm an old man, which is true. And that I'm a bit hard of hearing, also true. And I love the piano, all true. And I'm well behaved. Well, would you believe it, he's nice enough to invite me onstage. Must be I rate it. My force of personality."

That was probably it.

Our love story (what else?) languished for three or four months, during which time our hero was away in England on a lecture tour, the subject being the American labor and radical movements. How these lectures were arranged we could never quite figure out, nor did Bert care to explain. We put it down to a personal mystique; wherever he turned up, there he seemed destined to be. He would send small newspaper items concerning his appearances, including one from Glasgow that had his bewhiskered photograph. He was cast as an American scholar and luminary; we at home accepted that with pride.

We heard from stray postcards that he had been ill. Linda received several phone calls, one from Bert and others from friends abroad. He took to bed for a while; once he phoned to instruct Linda about sending some books, and where to send these same books in the event of his demise. "He'll kill himself over there," Linda said to me. "He can't refuse an opportunity to show off, whether it's down the block or halfway around the world. Invite him to lecture, he'll go. I have to admit I miss him. I'm fond of him and worry about him a lot. He's a man of too many talents and that can hurt you. He refuses to recognize age." She sighed, regarding me with her languorous smile that flashed with beauty (lucky Bert!) and continued, "But we often choose to suffer fools gladly, since the rest of us are boring, don't you think?"

"All I know is that we should keep that man on our street, and you too, Linda. We need all the class we can get here."

"The trouble is, dear friend, class doesn't pay the rent. Now, let me give you some special tea I brewed. Sensational."

When Bert returned, he was pale and thinner, and much quieter. Before long he began to put back some weight, owing to Linda's superior cooking. Next (what a movie!), a sight I could never have predicted: both of them out for a walk ... holding hands. And next again, I met them one afternoon on their way to a local movie, like two kids playing hookey from school.

He tried to explain this turnabout, always a little embarrassed. "I realized, when I was away, that she took good care of the apartment, it's cleaner than ever and most important, she got rid of those damned cats. It feels more like home."

Was he finally seduced by good cooking, and perhaps (only the gods would know) by sex? If handholding means anything, Linda may eventually tame even a tough fish like Bert for she was, and is, a woman of intelligence and exceptional use of grammar. Power to these mad darlings. Or, as Bert would prefer to say, "Power to the workers!"

Trek Into the Interior

Why do people smile when you say you're from Brooklyn—people who would react normally enough if you claimed to be from any of the other five boroughs that make up the city of New York?

Does Brooklyn have its own language? Do people here go around saying "hoit" for "hurt," "boid" for "bird," or "soda dish gimme the glim" for "so this dame gives me the eye?"

Why is the name of my town both a symbol of good will (Alaska) and a symbol of damnation (Manhattan)?

Is there something about us, an aura, an essence, a smell?

A short while ago, I set out to answer these questions. I began with the corner news vendor, seated deep inside his wooden shell, framed by photos of sadism, scientific horror, and young love. He greeted me with a half nod. He was a wiry man, hunched like an owl.

"Mike," I asked, "why do you live here in Brooklyn?"

"That's what I think about alla time," he said, "why I'm here, on this corner, for twenty years, when I coulda been in California, which I'm not."

I pondered this typical native response: feeling of being trapped, nostalgia for distant climes, yet a philosophical acceptance of Fate. Interesting, but only a beginning—and an oversimplification. To get at this whole complex matter, I would have to sample the Brooklyn character in its many local habitats.

So one bright morning, starting from my own habitat, Brooklyn Heights, I kissed my wife and child goodbye, started up my old heap, and off I raced for the open road.

I drove into Ben's Gas Station at the foot of Atlantic Avenue. I told Benny of my mission, and that I planned to do a story about what I discovered.

"A waste of gas. Stay home. Stay home and write about girls," he said. "People want to read about that."

Charlie, the attendant, announced that my gas tank was brimful with twelve gallons. "How much, Ben?" I asked.

He waved his hand idly. "Two dollars."

"How much I owe you all these years?"

"I'm waiting for you to drive up in a Cadillac; then you'll pay the full price, even for water and air."

He followed me to my car sagging in the sun like Don Quixote's old Rosinante. "Here, take this with you." He handed me a map of Brooklyn. "In case you get lost, who knows?"

As I left Ben's Garage, intent on my mission, I turned recklessly into a one-way street. At the bend in the street (there are many bent—or as they say elsewhere, curved—streets in Brooklyn) a police car waited, and as I came into view the red rotary light on its roof began to whirl. I stopped and a policeman emerged from the car and came toward me.

"Guess I was in a hurry to get on the Parkway." I felt my face cracking with the grin.

"Going to a hospital to have a baby, heh? Let's see your license."

I produced it. He examined it slowly: the torture method. He hummed a little tune, and then asked, "How come you passed the stop sign too?"

"Did I pass it?" I asked lamely.

"You passed it," he replied. He took out his summons book and a pen. "How do you want it, for 'passing a stop sign' or 'one-way street'?"

"Give me a break," I said glumly. "I just gassed up at Benny's—"

"You a friend of Benny?" And he waved me off with a mild warning. I turned my vehicle around and drove away at the ridiculous speed of twenty miles an hour. I was on my way.

The Belt Parkway feeds off Brooklyn Bridge and swings south along the shoreline—lower Manhattan and the Statue of Liberty opposite —leaving the panorama of harbor traffic as it dips into a roadway trough below street level, then rises sharply to a long overpass. For a brief moment, the eye scans a slightly tapered forest of rooftops that fades into a surrealist distance, the endless miles of symmetry in which two million inhabitants live. The Parkway slowly descends now to an above-street route, cutting southwest along miles of wharves, docks, terminal buildings and drydock sheds, then curving alongside railroad yards to the edge of the Narrows, the lower New York Bay through which all seagoing traffic must pass. This stretch (Shore Road) is broad and beautiful. Amid the monotonous groups of small houses and apartment buildings, remnants of the Mansion Era are still visible; for here, decades earlier, fronting the water on little knolls, baronial homes flourished. Now beauty and elegance have made way for need.

As I passed Fort Hamilton, the Bay widened, houses declined to a more ancient brick and frame, thinning into near-dilapidation; on the water side lay several rottings hulks. Ahead loomed a large Ferris wheel, a parachute drop—Coney Island. I turned off the Belt to search this southernmost part of Brooklyn for clues.

Coney, Mecca of the Elite at the turn of the century, has long since settled down as the Paradise of the Poor. Its drab interior streets of two-storied houses are hidden from the visitor, and it presents (in season) a garish face of frolic and games, hot-dog stands and custard marts, rides, steam baths, beaches and Fun after Dark. It probably has, in Nathan's, the largest and most rapid dispenser of hot dogs in the world. The place is tawdry, baroque, almost improvisational, as though it never expected to last another year and was surprised it had. The air was pulsing with faint music: a calliope, a jukebox, a barker's singsong.

Along one of the back-alley streets that is known as the "Bowery" I stopped at a novelty shop. "How long have you been living here?" I asked the man at the counter.

"Thirty years, close," he responded.

"Do you like it in Brooklyn?"

His eyebrows went up. "I have to like it?" Then, watching me eye a Kewpie doll, he said, "Today is bargain day. Sixty-nine cents you can have it for fifty." I bought the doll, and before I went a block the wind had whipped off half the feathers.

I filled up on hot dogs and potato chips and root beer. I rode the

Tornado and the Whip, but the exotic spirit of the place somehow did not touch me. I dropped in on a merchant whom I remembered from twenty-five years ago. (Coney was my first Brooklyn residence.) He recognized me, clucked his tongue in astonishment at seeing me alive. "How does it go on the outside? Where do you live?"

"I'm still in Brooklyn."

"You never left Brooklyn?" He clapped his forehead. "I knew I was never going to leave because I had a store, but why didn't *you* leave?"

"I didn't know where to go," I answered.

"Ah, to know where to go, that's the trick, my friend. But it's not too bad here. Everywhere it's the same; money kills you."

The afternoon was almost gone when I got into my car to drive home. At the entrance to the Belt, I stopped and looked ahead to the ribbon of concrete and steel stretching away to the east. I knew it went past Sheepshead Bay, Marine Park and the meadows and marshlands of Canarsie—then onward past the farthermost stretches of Brooklyn into Queens. Suddenly I knew it would be cowardice and evasion to pursue that path further—to drive *around* Brooklyn, rather than *through* it. Tomorrow I would have to strike into the interior.

The next day, I headed my vehicle into the mass of traffic, southward again. (The north seemed too improbable at the moment—*was* there a Brooklyn north?)

Much has been said about the Gowanus Canal. "Gowanus" is another of those contemptuous terms used by outsiders. I knew it was somewhere in South Brooklyn (which is not south but actually west, facing the Upper Bay across from Governors Island). I proceeded cautiously down Atlantic Avenue, turned into Columbia Street and entered Red Hook, barely a mile from the tree-lined, middle-class streets of Brooklyn Heights.

This was once a terror-ridden area, a bit of Italy transported to this country with its family law and ritual intact. Here the bloody battles of water-front unionism were once fought, and gangsterism with its killings was rampant. Now it seemed pacified. I rode through the battered streets swarming with kids, while the elders leaned out windows or sat in front of houses, chattering away in the sun. At the end of these streets, ships were unloading cargo from all over the world.

I found the Gowanus, a thin strip of oily water, stagnant as a pond. I wouldn't give a duck a chance in that water; it looked like sure death. On both banks of the Canal, across its single bridge and overhead where the subway rose from the ground like a worm, traffic moved. I crossed the bridge and walked down to the water's edge where two small tugs were tied up. There was a sand-and-gravel company nearby, and I walked over and poked my head inside the door.

A burly man rose from behind the desk. He was Irish and cocky. I told him I was exploring Brooklyn and would like to know about the Gowanus—which certainly puzzled him. "Not many cities have canals," I ventured, "and a canal, you might say, gives a place character."

He grinned. "It used to be called Lavender Lake. It sure don't smell lavender."

"Is it still in operation?"

He scratched his head. "It's in operation, all right." He called back inside the building. "Hey, Bill, how far does the creek go?"

"Around Carroll maybe, or Sackett, somewhere up there," a voice called back.

"About a mile maybe, the whole works. We haul sand and cement from the Erie Basin. Someone got an option on this canal fifty years ago." He called inside again, "Who in hell owns this canal, Bill?" The voice answered, "Whatsamatter, anyone there want to buy it?"

I hung around a while, hoping to see some barge traffic, but didn't, and finally took off, threading my way slowly south through the sections called Borough Park and Bensonhurst, which, together with Flatbush, make up the heaviest residential concentrations.

Further southward—sudden open areas, empty lots, auto junkyards. Then I discovered a farm—right under the BMT Elevated line on McDonald Avenue. It was not much more than an acre, but it was skillfully planted. Rows of beans, lettuce, tomatoes and asparagus took up every foot of space. Overhead, on trellises, were grapevines, heavily weighted. Angelo, the farmer, was on his knees setting new tomato plants. He said he was seventy-five, and sixty years a farmer. He was agile, witty, and eager to talk.

"I farm in old country, Sicily. The air, the air! Here is no air! But in morning, five o'clock, is good air. Man from next door get up early watch me to work, he start to feel better because of good air. Farms all gone. Was many farms near here. Avenue P, Neck Road. Freight car come to pick up grapes long time. Now all sell for houses. People like houses, not farm. Everything change in Brooklyn." He paused while the elevated train clattered above our heads.

"How long have you been farming here?"

"Forty years. I don't sell. They come all time, want to buy my small land. I don't sell. When I die, end of my farm. Soon end of all farms, everybody die." He grinned, and turned to his work.

I drove past a cemetery, past a plumbing supply house with bathtubs and sinks all over the sidewalk, past gas stations and interminable streets of orderly houses. It was warm; a haze hung over the roadway; I was losing my sense of direction.

I stopped at a hot dog vendor and realized my confusion had been due to hunger. The small outdoor stand looked familiar. Of course . . . I was just around the corner from Ebbets Field. This was now a ghostly place, now that the Dodgers had gone west. Did anyone miss them, I wondered?

In Brooklyn someone is always reading your thoughts, and it hardly surprised me when the hot dog man spoke. "Sure is quiet since the Dodgers left. They were a lousy team, even when they won the pennant, but there was noise around here. You could hear it from here, a block away, that yell which meant Duke Snider struck out on a bad pitch or Carl Furillo made a great catch or Pee Wee laid down a bunt. Ah-h-h, I hope they all get asthma out in L.A. They left us just when they were getting real lousy, so good riddance, but alla same, they were great ballplayers and I still remember Gil Hodges hitting a grand slam against the Giants. I hated the Giants. There's nobody left to hate any more. Brooklyn is changed. We have soccer here now. Soccer! In *Brooklyn!*"

I jogged over to the Botanical Gardens nearby, thinking that Nature would lift my spirits. I ran into three pickets at the gates. Nature on Strike—where else but in Brooklyn?

"Who's taking care of the flowers while you guys are out?" I asked.

A chubby man with a placard said, "They take care of themselves."

The others laughed. Another man informed me that the strikers were skilled professionals. "Most people think that gardeners are just shovel men. This is not true. I, for example, am a Master of Horticulture. I have degrees from Riga, Munich and Cornell."

A policeman came up, checked the phone box and strolled over. "Hi, Gus," he greeted the picket. "Anybody cross the picket line?"

The chubby one replied, "We have little old rich ladies come in every day to water the flowers in the hothouse. Ain't that nice?"

"Should give you guys more money, if they was honest. Tell ya the truth, nuthin's honest in this city. It hoits me to say it."

I distinctly heard him say "hoit." Had I at last stumbled upon a genuine Brooklyn type? I remarked it was nice to see a nonbelligerent cop watching a picket line. He said cheerfully, "Some cops know the book, but are bad in human relations. You need human relations. Them old days when cops usta beat up pickets is gone. Pickets is people, y'know? Usta be they'd send drinkers and shake-down artists for picket patrol. Now they send the best of us; this ain't no foul-ball area. They pick the best." He felt the knot on his tie. "I shouldn't carry on this conversation wid you; the sergeant wouldn't like it. I'm not supposed to talk. I am a deterrent to crime, just *to be seen.*"

"Is this your regular beat?" I asked.

"I'm from Williamsburg. I'm here on loan, you might say."

A car pulled over to the curb with a New Jersey license. The driver called out, "How do I get to Prospect Park West, Officer?"

"I'm not from this neighborhood, pal," answered the cop. The car pulled away. "Those Jersey guys are really ignorant once they leave Jersey, y'notice?"

I visited the Sculpture Court of the nearby Brooklyn Museum, a large, high-domed area with a center fountain, then strolled through an adjoining wing. "This time of year," an amiable guard there told me, "you don't get the crowds. People are out riding in cars or in the parks."

I asked him what it was like to have a museum job. He replied, "You couldn't retire on the salary. Libraries, museums, same thing. All that money for highways so's people can be on the move. But no money so's people can stand still and read a book or look at a painting. Fine reflection on modern life, heh?"

Is a guard kept busy with questions, I asked him. "The biggest question is from the ladies wanting to know where's the Ladies' Room." He sighed. "Then you get kids who mark up a statue, like signing their names on a bosom. You feel like tossing 'em in the fountain, but you are polite and lecture them on vandalism, the little monsters. Still, lots of people come here, which proves Brooklyn ain't all gin mills."

I was uneasy about continuing north, but once I crossed Atlantic Avenue I felt more relaxed. Atlantic gave me a sense of place; I knew I lived off one end of it. According to my map, I was approaching Williamsburg.

A street sign rang a bell. Kosciusko! Kosciusko Street of the ancient joke about the horse that dropped dead on that street and the cop came by to write an official report but couldn't spell Kosciusko so he had the horse dragged a block over to Hart. I turned into Kosciusko and noticed several men seated against the wall of a small factory. I parked the car.

"Watch out," one of them said. "The cops here are ticket-happy."

"I'm not staying long," I said. "Just looking around." That remark silenced them. "I'm driving through on my way to Williamsburg." That seemed to make things worse. Then, with a nervous laugh: "I saw the name Kosciusko Street, y'know, and I figured—"

The man who'd warned me astonished me by saying, "You mean that joke about dragging the horse from Kosciusko to Hart? Except the next street isn't Hart, it's DeKalb, Pulaski, then Hart. So even if the cop dragged the dead horse a block over to DeKalb he couldn't'a spelled it anyway if he was a Brooklyn cop." The others agreed. "And another thing," the man continued, "you notice they have a new street sign up there? Because for years they had it spelled Koscuisko, *ui* instead of *iu*, maybe a hundred years till somebody noticed it, and they changed it right."

"How long have you been living in Brooklyn?" I asked him.

"Thirty—forty years, I forget. I planned to leave lots of times but here I am. Even when I die...because they'll probably bury me here, with all the cemeteries. Brooklyn is fulla cemeteries."

"I got some land in the Poconos," said the second man.

"Pennsylvania," said the third man, scornfully.

I decided to put a crucial question. "Do you guys think there is a special Brooklyn character?" A cold silence. The first man spat and said, "My idea of the Brooklyn character is when you're parking in a No Parking zone for a minute to go around the corner to the Traffic Court to pay a parking ticket, and while you're gone a cop puts another one on your car, and you keep on living. That's true Brooklyn, pal."

I said I was headed for Williamsburg and then Greenpoint. "Williamsburg is half-dead and Greenpoint is all-dead," he commented.

I swung up Union and passed a very old building that manufactured wire (it was 110 years old), and before long I was in Williamsburg, a tightly congested area of several immigrant generations, including a recent influx of Hasidim. It had a few housing projects, but the place lacked the openness and freedom of the southern part of the borough. I followed Union to Manhattan Avenue and into Greenpoint. I had reached the upper end of Brooklyn. At the northern tip, across Newtown Creek, was Queens. Along the opposite shore, locomotives pulled grimy freight cars. I couldn't see any Queens streets, but the map said they were there.

I backed away from Queens and wandered around Greenpoint Avnenue. It struck me as having the quality of a small town: I saw an old church, an old synagogue, a closed mission, and an 1880 store front.

"Yes," agreed a bystander, "it is a small town. All of these sections in Brooklyn—Williamsburg, Flatbush, Canarsie—all were once little towns. Here it was fancy once. We had a ferry went straight across to 23rd Street, New York. We had a political boss who kept the neighborhood strict and clean. When a political boss dies you go downhill. Greenpoint is going down. I like it, but it isn't the same Greenpoint as when I came here thirty years ago."

After a while I parked my car and went into a bar. A barmaid was serving drinks. I sat down and had a few beers. I had no idea where I was; it was getting dark. I asked the barmaid how to get back to Borough Hall. She asked an amiable yellow-toothed trucker seated next to me. He eyed me slowly, and finally got me into focus. "You mean walkin' or ridin'?"

"I have a car," I said.

"How did you get here by car?"

I no longer remembered my route, and opened a map. He leaned back perilously. "You drove here with a *map*?" There was a stirring among the line of drinkers.

I mumbled a reply. The trucker insisted on buying me a drink, and I could not tolerably refuse. We had several. Brooklyn, for the first time that day, started to look rosy, really started to take on a character: a haven for the tired and poor, a place for people to come home at night, a breeding ground for philosophers and poets.

The trucker droned on at my side, "...because what the hell you can't take it with you if yer goin' and we all are, well if I was you, fella, I'd go to the end of Devoe'n' turn right on Manhattan until—"

A listener cut in, "You can't turn right, Jack, it's one-way."

"Did I say turn on Manhattan?"

"You did, Mac."

"I musta meant Union."

"And he turns *left* on Union cause he is goin' south, right?"

"Yeah, but I was gonna steer him to the Parkway. He goes right, then left on Metropolitan which runs into the Belt."

The word Belt roused me. "I was on the Belt yesterday," I said, surprised at how slowly I formed the words. "I don't want the Belt any more. I want the interior, y'see?"

"Where you wanna go, pal?" asked the trucker.

"Borough Hall section," I said, downing another of several beers which appeared mysteriously before me. "Where the Hall of Records is."

"You cannot beat the Belt, son, which runs out of Park into Tillary which takes you to where that statue of Ward Beecher which is Borough Hall—am I getting through?"

"Would you like something to eat?" asked the barmaid.

"Thank you," I said. "Yes."

"We don't sell food here, but I have some cold cuts on the ice, and seein' you got to drive home, it might fix you up." She rapidly cut some ham and prepared a sandwich. "You mean you never been to Greenpoint before?"

"No, ma'am."

"I'll tell you, I never been to New York till I was over twenty. My mother wouldn't allow me, and I never been there since. It goes to prove."

I did not know what it proved, but it did. It surely and firmly did, I thought, as I munched my sandwich, wondering how the rest of Brooklyn was getting along. I thought of my wife and child far to the south. I began to sing.

I decided to leave my car in Greenpoint overnight, being slightly green and unsteady. I found a cab and said to the driver, "You can let me off in front of Ward Beecher. Yeah, the guy on the pedestal, Borough Hall, where the main Post Office is. God Bless the Post Office!"

"You don't remember the one-cent post card, do you?" he asked.

"No," I said, "but I remember the five-cent post card. And the ten-cent airmail. And the special delivery stamp with a guy riding a bicycle on it." I controlled a wild desire to cry.

A half-hour later, I was walking down the far end of Hicks Street where a newly opened, dimly candlelit cafe was whooping it up with a poetry reading. The room was crowded. A small bar (Cokes and cider only) served the customers. Beards were prominent. Photos of Henry Miller on the wall. Nudes (on wall).

A poet was reading aloud:

> Sat I
> Sandy dry
> Near the skin of the sea . . .

I stayed awhile, then left. It was almost midnight when I approached my house. The sound of recorder music reached my ears. It came from my neighbor's apartment. He answered my knock. "Come in," he said. "We are having a little Bach and Buxtehude, also some Purcell." Seated in a circle, four recorder players nodded politely and resumed the concert.

The music comforted me. This, too, was Brooklyn, I reminded myself, where men did not fear to gather with nonconformist instruments. Threats by some neighbors against midnight soirees, even visits by the police acting upon complaints, failed to shake the determination of this recorder group.

"The recorder is a noble instrument," a player, Carl Cowl, explained to me. "We will not yield to TV barbarians. They may call us piccolo players in their ignorance, they may jeer at us, but we shall continue to play our music in this street."

The next morning was sunny. A mass of polluted air hovered darkly over Manhattan, but that was not my concern. Before going to pick up my car, I took a slow walk through the neighborhood, marveling at the neatness and compactness of its streets, the small but resolute trees, and the optimism reflected on faces. My anxiety of yesterday faded— obviously, the character of a place depended on weather; I was a fool not to realize it.

I stopped in at the Montague Street library, whose librarians are the salt of the earth, and I went to make some notes in a private room which the library allows me to use. I was interrupted by the Turkish cleaning woman whose greeting was always the same: "Are you writing that *same story?*" All my years of work in the library seemed to her one continuous story; perhaps, uncannily, she was right. "I will pray for you to sell your story because you are a good boy."

Someone always prays for you in Brooklyn.

I met a book dealer I know outside the library. "I'm not sure if it's good or bad, what's happening," he said. "Take Montague Street, this whole area, used to be classy. Now it's no class. People have moved in from all over. I've been here for thirty years. Used to be in the old days, on a Sunday people would dress up and just walk up and down the street. Now they go out in a car and kill somebody. You never saw a woman without a hat; now you're lucky if they got a whole dress on. Dignity and decorum, that's what has vanished. Dignity and decorum. Brooklyn used to be top drawer—now it's bottom, and the bottom's falling out. Maybe the bottom's falling out of the world."

His voice trailed off. He lit a cigarette. "There was mansions all along Clinton and Willoughby Avenue—millionaires. Now they got housing projects. You know Spencer Place and Bedford? Folger used to live there, hundred years ago. He set up the Folger Shakespeare Library in Washington. Anderson lived around there; he was a great art collector. The Pratts and Singers gave the place real class; Pouch of Standard Oil—the Fifth Avenue names were here. It lost its character. Everybody started to move in." He shook his head sadly. "You don't like to say it's gettin' seedy, but it's the truth."

Change was a key word. Yet, within change, the stubborn resistance of ancient values. On State Street, I saw an old brownstone building that housed the Islamic Mission of America.

While not too distant, the oldest synagogue in Brooklyn, Congregation Beith Israel Anshei Emis—known as the Kane Street Synagogue —was having its services, enduring well over a century within a changing city. The borough is rich in churches and its architecture; some churches have been converted into co-ops or cultural centers such as St. Ann's, reflecting community pressures and change. Was the meaning merely change? And who would judge the loss or gain?

Later that day, I went back to pick up my car. I had made a note of its exact location in Greenpoint. The subway took me there. I turned the corner into the street—but the car was gone. I checked the street; the street was there and the bar. Then I noticed the NO PARKING TOW-AWAY ZONE sign. I had fallen into the most ignominious police trap. My groan must have brought the barmaid to the door. "Hello," she said. "My husband and I pushed your car into the driveway. We thought you maybe never made it back to your house last night." Her smile—I cannot describe it to the outsider—lifted my heart.

"How'd you get into the car? It was locked."

"My son goes to Technical High and he knows how to open any car door. He's very bright." She led me to the driveway. I thanked her and drove off.

I nosed my craft southeasterly, into the Ridgewood section, skirting the cemetery of the Evergreens beyond whose stones lay mysterious Queens, stretching endlessly and terrifyingly eastward. I approached Atlantic Avenue which cuts an east-west swath across the borough. Then, without knowing why, I turned east and was speeding toward Queens.

I had to touch Queens soil—some psychic impulse drove me on. I clipped along Atlantic. My heart quickened; I felt a soaring sensation; no, rather a sensation of approaching dread. The streets ticked off, and then—I was over! I was in Queens. Gone were the solid masses of homes; now patches of green separated them. Gone were people in front of stores. Gone were the signs of commerce and industry: no men in undershirts sitting on boxes during a work break, no trucks backing into loading areas. A peculiar silence or, rather, lack of turmoil. The storekeepers were inside their stores and people inside their houses. Those men and women I saw on the streets were dressed as though they were going to graduation exercises. Dignity and decorum—they had it here.

I called out to a parked taxi, "Where am I, Mac?" and he answered politely, "This is Queens."

I turned and raced back, past the neat blocks, the strange faces—I was over! Take me to thy bosom. If I forget thee, O Breuckelen, let my right hand wither!

The sky darkened as I headed into the buzzing human hive straight down Atlantic Avenue, with its tawdry vistas, its racking elevated; the streets of the poor, past the flimsy Negro shacks, the small factories, a gas-station sign announcing IRVING IS BACK, the Bedford Avenue Armory, the high twin spires of a church. Across Flatbush Avenue I drove, dodging pedestrians and dogs, missing a fire truck, rushing through a cloud of pigeons—and it began to rain.

One of my rear wheels hissed and sagged. I was getting a flat. But I did not stop. I was not far from the sanctuary of Ben's Garage, where I was known, where I would be welcomed. I limped that last half mile, aware I was ruining a tire.

Ahead, off the edge of Atlantic, the docks and winking lights of the river barges. Under the cursed Belt overpass, I coasted in. Ben was there hatless, discussing a *Racing Form* with a cop in a patrol car.

"Ben," I shouted. I cut my motor.

"Hello," he answered. "You need a beer. Come in." We went inside the office. "So here you are. You really rode all over Brooklyn? What did you find—uranium? I bet you found nothing."

"I'm not sure, Ben."

"What do you mean you're not sure?"

"I have to be honest about it."

Ben stared at me. "Who says not to be honest? Just write that it's a nice place here with lots of pretty girls, friendly people, a nice place to live. It's true, if you want to be honest. We're as good as anybody." And he laughed.

That laugh confirmed a thought forming in my mind. He was laughing at himself and defending himself at the same time. That is why people laugh at Brooklynites. We are in their eyes the borough of the underdog, and we are receptive to that image—we may well be it. We flaunt our lower-class polyglot origin; it is in our bones ("We're as good as anybody"). We still retain, generations later, that peculiar extroversion and vitality of the immigrant. It may explain our friendliness and tolerances, and the clannishness of neighborhood. It may explain our disdain of grammar even into the Americanized generations.

Spreading out or moving elsewhere as our economic status changed, to be followed by new underdog waves, the blacks and more recently the Puerto Ricans, we always knew, unconsciously, that this was a "beginning" place. We know, today, that those on their way up the ladder never move into Brooklyn; they move out of it into Manhattan, Westchester, Queens, or the reaches of Long Island. But some of us have in our blood, I think, the fierce pride of Those Who Stayed. And many stayed all their lives.

It's not only that we are receptive to the image of the underdog; we even anoint our heroes in that light. Where else would a baseball team like the Brooklyn Dodgers, with its pennant and World Series victories, be proudly referred to as "Bums"? Are they called "bums" in Los Angeles? No. That Johnny-come-lately city would never see it that way. Los Angeles has never truly suffered.

Brooklyn is a lot of small towns without boundaries; it is definitely a place, as well as a *mystique*. To live in it is to love it—which does not mean you might not be secretly planning to break out. But those who do are never happy; I have received more than one letter of remorse from impulsive emigrants who went to (O the madness)—California!

Charlie's voice broke into my meditation. "Man needs a new tire and tube on this beat-up heap."

And Ben answering grandly, "Put it on. And use fresh air, no cheap air!"

I was suddenly very tired. "Mind if I use your phone, Ben?"

"No long distance, please."

"No long distance. Just a couple of blocks." I dialed, watching the rain outside drift down across the oncoming night. Traffic was speeding by on the elevated Belt toward nearby Brooklyn Bridge, whose outline I knew so well. And those lines of Hart Crane again returning as music of that vision:

Then, with inviolate curve, forsake our eyes
As apparitional as sails that cross
Some page of figures to be filed away . . .

"Hello?" It was my wife's voice.
"It's me," I said. "I'm home."

Passing Through

A dry cool morning, possibly Autumn (the seasons in Brooklyn are not clearly divided.) I step out into the steet, slapping my hips to make sure the guns are buckled on. It's a purely mythic gesture, an urban reflex, could be any civilized American city. Yet each of us can rightfully feel embattled, even on a peaceful morning. We'll pass over the news of a hurricane on the move, an unruly volcano, toxic waste undermining the Appalachian range, nature's revenge everywhere, and come to this day, the small events thereof that trouble and sustain us.

Who is it at this hour crossing my path? Not the black cat of good fortune, but the paragon of animals, a man. More specifically, the rental agent of our building come to check on a tenant complaint.

"Up early, are you?" he says with an actor's joviality. "I thought you writers slept all day."

"This happens to be a work day, John. I'm out to buy a typewriter ribbon. You haven't got one on you by any chance?"

He laughs cautiously, not being sure if he should. "So, we haven't spoke for weeks. When are you going to leave?"

"Leave where?"

"Your apartment."

"I'm not going anywhere."

John grinned in reply. As agent for the brownstone where I lived for a third of a century, he was friendly, sardonic, with a flash of toughness occasionally showing. "We'll set you up somewhere else just as nice." It was cat-mouse, except neither was sure who was which, it had been going on for some years. Landlord-tenant stalemate. War under the general heading of gentrification. "You think about it," he said genially.

"No chance," I answered. "I'm staying."

"We need the apartment." He guffawed, as Goliath might have at David. "We're going to get you out, all you old-timers. There's big money ready to move in. No hard feelings."

"Always a pleasure," I replied, at my polite best.

He winked. "Have a nice day."

Change in the neighborhood. A restless influx of souls. The upward mobility scramble. Enter fast food, boutiques, cash machines, and ice cream everywhere. Exit a shoemaker one week, a tailor shop the next, a bakery is missing, then a small bookstore famous for browsing . . . and can the poet laureate be far behind?

I begin my chores of the day. A small purchase at the stationery store, a typewriter ribbon. Marvin asks how many ribbons I use in a month. I reply that it depends upon how hot the story is; he accepts the answer with a chuckle. I stop by at the Xerox emporium where Sid keeps an eye on neighborhood writers and blesses each completed manuscript. He cannot understand why we don't turn out the big money stuff; I can't either. I stock up on stamps at the GPO, my local Chartres with its eloquent architecture: post cards, first class stamps, a strip of airmails, and a new issue with Emily Dickinson (bless her) featured. I next look in at the branch library where Sylvia of the Business Section inquires about my poetry. I reply that I may be into a new style, wondering to myself if it's true. They all like hearing good news about me, and I suppose I do too. I'm haunted by those whirling brushes off the ground, though still singing an aria. Yes, that must be me.

I walk back to the house, into a room where my day begins. At the window I lean out over the low rooftops where the small dark-leaved maple will soon slip into its winter death, with resurrection merely half a year away.

I stand and look out at the landscape, the landscape looks in at me. We wish each other well. Time here is not measured in years, but decades, these single days repeated, lost, fated to be lived within this boundary of streets and the lives thereof. The trees will be witness, or a bird flying through the gritty air on the way to sunshine.

I move into the time of myself, this room where my day begins and ends and begins again.